ACTIVITIES

Scientific Inquiry

AGES 7-11

PAULA HAMMOND

Author
Paula Hammond

Editors
Nicola Morgan
Caroline Carless

Project Editor
Fabia Lewis

Series Designers
Anthony Long
Joy Monkhouse

Designer
Catherine Perera

Illustrations
Gemma Hastilow

**Published by Scholastic Ltd,
Villiers House,
Clarendon Avenue,
Leamington Spa,
Warwickshire CV32 5PR**

www.scholastic.co.uk

Text © 2007 Paula Hammond
© 2007 Scholastic Ltd

Designed using Adobe Indesign

Printed by Tien Wah Press Ltd, Singapore

1 2 3 4 5 6 7 8 9   7 8 9 0 1 2 3 4 5 6

British Library Cataloguing-in-Publication Data

A catalogue record for this book is available from the
British Library.

ISBN 978-0439-94501-1

Contents

Introduction

Children are naturally inquisitive, with a desire to learn about the world around them. In fact, they're instinctual scientists! While they may not consciously label it as such, almost everything that catches their imagination, from games consoles to animatronic dinosaurs, are a product of science. Yet, by the time they reach school, many children have already learned to be wary of science - often viewed as a bastion of dry facts and dull equations. This book has been written to offer an inspirational introduction to the creative possibilities of Key Stage 2 science. My focus throughout will be to show that, in addition to being useful, science can also be surprising, stimulating and fun.

How do I use this book?

This book is divided into five chapters, each containing six experiments, which are designed to be achievable by children across the Key Stage. Support and extension ideas are included in every activity to ensure all children are able to participate. Each experiment is introduced using a series of memorable characters, stories and role-play situations. Although these experiments are written as lesson plans, there is more than enough work in each one to provide activities for several lessons. This gives the opportunity to cherry pick ideas, or spilt the activities into several, shorter, linked lessons, depending on which approach is more appropriate for the age and ability of the children. Individual experiments can also be used to build into a body of themed work on specific topics. Further information on this is given in the introduction to each chapter.

Six photocopiable pages are provided per chapter. These offer ideas for differentiated follow-up work, plus a range of templates on which children can record their findings: from encyclopaedia entries to virtual web pages; nature diaries to documentary storyboards.

Objectives

Although there is some overlap, each chapter in this book focuses on a number of specific areas of scientific investigation:

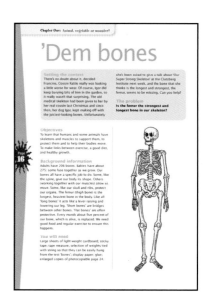

Chapter 1 - Humans and other living things.
Chapter 2 - Green plants and the environment.
Chapter 3 - Grouping, sorting and classifying materials; Forces and motion; Our planet and beyond.

Chapter 4 - Mixing and changing materials; Forces and motion; Electricity.
Chapter 5 - Light and sound; Electricity; Scientific enquiry.

As they work through each chapter, the children should also develop a knowledge and understanding of scientific techniques by exploring scientific ideas, planning experiments and, obtaining and presenting evidence, using a range of resources and approaches. With this in mind, the final two experiments in Chapter 5 are intended to

give children the chance to draw on and consolidate the research, investigation and evaluation skills that they have developed from participating in the activities in this book.

Background information

The science has been kept as simple and as accessible as possible for Key Stage 2 children. However, included on every activity page is a box of background information, which offers a brief overview of the topic being covered. It is hoped that this will be a useful aide-memoir whilst offering additional detail for those children who enjoy a challenge. Scientific language definitions are also provided, which highlight any new words the children may have learned during the activity.

Investigations and observations

Not all of the activities in this book fit into the traditional concept of science 'experiments'. The aim is to show children that science permeates every part of their lives, with practical real world applications. So, during the course of their work, they may find themselves carrying out research and development, product testing, model building, surveys or taking on the role of forensics experts at the scene of a crime. Throughout, however, children are

encouraged to work together, to pool their ideas and share their deliberations and discoveries. Therefore, each activity is divided into three distinct sections that will hopefully help children get to grips with the topic in their own way.

Discussion and research

This section acts as an introduction to the topic. Children are encouraged to exchange information and ideas before the experiment begins, using teacher-led questions and answers, pop quizzes, role-plays, puzzles and even magic shows, to stimulate debate and investigation.

Obtaining evidence

This offers children the chance to put their ideas to the test and discover answers to questions for themselves, by taking part in a practical experiment or watching a teacher-led demonstration. Where possible, experiments are intended to be collaborative, and it is suggested that, once children understand what's required of them, they be allowed to take ownership of the activity, at least as much as is practical, by choosing their own equipment and debating ideas and approaches with their peers.

Drawing together

The final section rounds up activities.

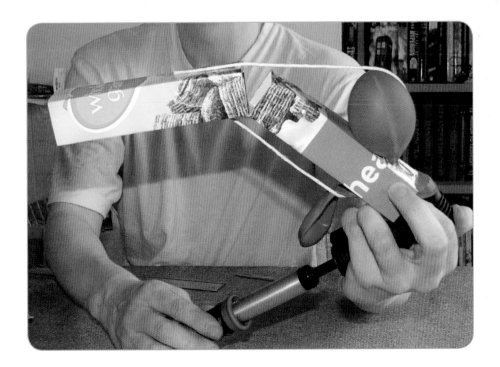

Children are challenged to question, consider and share their findings with the rest of the group. This often involves using unusual and memorable techniques, such as presenting their findings in the form of a television science show or a report to the head of the Secret Service.

Support

All of the experiments are designed to be suitable for children across the Key Stage. However, you may find that the following activities are more appropriate for younger children:

Sourcing equipment

In writing this book I have tried to avoid making experiments too prescriptive. The aim is that every activity can be carried out, whatever the setting, using whatever equipment is at hand - whether that be empty jam-jars or laboratory glass beakers. It is therefore recommended that you test out experiments before each lesson to determine the exact quantities and measurements that work best for you. Where specific equipment is recommended, you will find suggestions for the best places to source them, or ideas for suitable alternatives.

Safety

Finally, although these experiments are designed to be as safe as possible, children can be notoriously unpredictable! They will need to be supervised carefully throughout,

encouraged to be thorough and methodical in their work, to test and re-test observations, to use appropriate equipment in a careful manner and, above all, to be safe in their scientific practice.

Chapter One

Animal, vegetable or monster?

The six activities in this chapter give children the opportunity to explore a variety of topics that come under the banner of 'Life processes and living things'. The children will be involved in debates, games, model making, data gathering and experimentation.

We begin with **It lives... or does it?**, which encourages children to grow their own crystals and then determine whether they are living or non-living. The activity introduces the idea that, in science, there are often rules or criteria that can help us to prove or disprove a theory. As the crystals develop, they can be seen to fulfil some of the criteria for living things: they appear to eat (the solution reduces), they seem to reproduce and they grow. But are they alive?

In **Just like Mummy?,** children are introduced to the concept of heredity: exploring the physical similarities and differences that we share with our relatives. The activity focuses on data gathering, using a 'Whose Baby?' quiz and a family survey to show how facts and figures can be used in science to support our ideas.

Pump it up! looks at the wonders of the human body; specifically our muscles - how they work and how they can be affected by exercise and a good diet. The activity also introduces the concept that scientists often use simplified models of the real thing to test their ideas. Children are given the chance to create their own working Robo Arm and draw up blueprints of their completed design.

Stoking the engine, **Potent potions** and **'Dem bones** are more traditional experiments, each with a hypothesis to be proved or disproved through testing and exploration. **'Dem bones** looks at our skeleton and investigates which bone is the longest and strongest. It can be used in conjunction with **Pump it up!** for a linked body of work on movement. **Stoking the engine** explores the heart and blood circulation, and compares heart rates at rest and at work. Children can be given the opportunity to make their own model heart. **Potent potions** focuses on the functions and care of teeth, with children taking on the role of Product Development Teams to test the effects of various foods, and mystery Potion X, on our teeth.

It lives... or does it?

Setting the context

Deep within Castle Clutz lies the secret laboratory of Francine Stein. Here, away from prying eyes, she tests out some of her most brilliant, bizarre and baffling ideas. Luckily, her experiments don't entail any grizzly trips to the graveyard to pick up spare parts; just some simple household items. However, Francine's latest experiment, growing crystals, is giving her a bit of a headache. She thinks, from the way the crystals behave, that they might actually be alive. Could she be right?

Problem

Are crystals really alive?

Objectives

To know that all living things grow, eat, reproduce and respond to their surroundings.
To know that some solids dissolve in liquids to make solutions, while some do not.
To understand how to recover dissolved solids by evaporation.

Background information

Simple crystals can be made from salt or sugar solutions, but these can take weeks to form. Borax crystals begin to form within a day, allowing the process to be observed easily and then recorded. Crystals are solids with a symmetrical, repeating shape. Boiled water is used to make the solution because the water molecules are further apart, allowing more borax to be dissolved. As it cools, the molecules close up and excess borax is deposited, forming crystals.

You will need

A selection of interesting items for discussion, such as: yeast (activated or inactivated); caterpillar chrysalis; stone covered in algae; match; bath bomb; slinky; fossil.

Per group: borax*; boiling water; beaker or disposable cup; spoon; pencil; length of string or a pipe cleaner; food colouring; disposable gloves; thermometer (optional); photocopiable page 20.

* Borax is a cleaning product often found in chemists. Online retailers include Dri-Pak (www.dri-pak.co.uk), Lawsons (www.lawsonshop.co.uk) and The Green Shop (www.greenshop.co.uk).

Safety Borax can be an irritant so, as with all chemicals, avoid direct contact with skin. Boiling water and steam can burn; supervise children closely.

Preparation

Set up a display of the living and non-living objects. Set aside space and equipment for demonstrations such as a bath bomb. Make labels for children to add to the display: 'Living' and 'Non-living'.

Discussion and research

● Encourage children to examine the items on display, discussing how they look, feel and smell. How many of the items do they think are alive? Vote on each and then label them 'Living' or 'Non-living'. Encourage the children to discuss their decisions where there is no clear consensus.

● In science there are often rules to help us prove or disprove a theory. Scientists classify living things as those which: Grow, Eat, Reproduce and Respond to their surroundings, GERR for short!

● Even when using GERR it isn't always easy to tell what's alive and what isn't. The flame on a burning match moves and seems to feed on the wood and grow. If we add fuel, it even 'reproduces'. Chemical reactions like the bath bomb placed in water can make objects seem alive. The chrysalis contains a living creature, but isn't alive itself. (It could be allowed to develop in a suitable tank for further study). Yeast is alive, although scientists can't decide if it's a plant or an animal.

● Using the GERR **criteria**, consider again which items from the display are alive, changing the labels where necessary.

● Finally, reveal the correct answers. *How well did we do?*

Obtaining evidence

● It's easy to see why Francine is confused about whether the crystals she's made are really alive. To help her, we need to reproduce her experiment:

1. Fill a beaker $\frac{3}{4}$ full with boiling water.
2. Add a spoonful of borax. Stir until completely dissolved.
3. Stir in more borax, until a residue can be seen on the bottom of the beaker.
4. Add a drop food colouring. You now have a **saturated solution**.
5. Hang the string from a glass rod laid across the beaker. The string should hang into the solution, but shouldn't touch the bottom of the beaker.
6. Label, leave and observe.

● Help the children to choose and set out their equipment.

● You may want to use measuring jugs, a thermometer and count the number of spoonfuls of borax. This will ensure that the solutions the children make are all the same. Alternatively, allow them to experiment for

themselves, recording what they did for comparison. However, avoid disappointments by allowing children to repeat experiments that don't work.

Drawing together

● Encourage the children to display their crystals to the class and explain what they did and what happened during their experiments.

● Draw out: What equipment they used; what unusual things they saw/heard/ smelled; where they think the crystals came from; how pleased they are with the results; what they would do differently next time.

● From what they have observed, do they think that the crystals are alive?

● How well do crystals fulfil the GERR criteria? Draw up two lists, 'For' and 'Against', before a final class vote.

Support
Use the display and the photocopiable sheet to introduce and reinforce the idea that some things are living while others are not.

Extension
Help the children explore how changes affect experimental results. For example, using cold water rather than hot or replacing borax with alum powder (sold as potassium aluminium sulphate).

Scientific language
criteria - rules used to help make a decision
saturated - when a solution has taken in as much of another substance as it can
solution - a mixture of two or more substances

Just like Mummy?

Setting the context

Queen Smelliefetti was Francine's Mummy. Well, really she belonged to Uncle Digemup's Museum, she'd stood in the corner of Francine's lab for so long that she was like one of the family. The problem was that there were no paintings of Smelliefetti so Francine could only guess what she looked like beneath those layers of bandages. Then, one day, Francine learned about heredity: how children take after their parents. So, she figured, if she could find paintings of Smelliefetti's sons and daughters, then she'd have a good idea what the Queen herself was like....

The problem

Do all family members really look alike?

Objectives

To understand the main stages of the human life cycle.
To know that all living things grow, eat, reproduce and respond to their surroundings. To make links between living things and the environment in which they are found.

Background information

Sexual reproduction needs male and female sex **cells** to create new life. Our physical traits are determined by bio-chemical instructions, called **genes**, carried in these cells. Half come from mum's egg and half from dad's sperm. So we look like our parents but aren't exact copies. Some genes are recessive and less likely to be passed on. They may skip a generation meaning we look more like gran than mum. Dominant genes are more likely to result in visible traits. People from the same place also often have similar traits because they share the same environment. Ultimately, however, regardless of appearances, we're all related because we're the same species: Homo sapien.

You will need

Per child: family photographs; completed copy of photocopiable page 21.

Preparation

Hand out copies of the photocopiable sheet to be taken home and completed. Ask parents/relatives* to choose two photographs, one of themselves when they were the same age as their child, and one of their child. Parents should write their names on the back of each photograph in pencil and place in a sealed envelope to be handed in before the activity begins. Mount the photograph of the parents (using mounts to avoid damaging the photographs) onto long strips of display paper, such as sentence strips.
* If you have children in your class who are adopted or not in regular contact with their biological parents then you may want to change the focus of the activity to avoid distress. Use the photographs and photocopiable sheet to introduce the theme of 'similarities' and 'differences' instead.

Discussion and research

● Begin by discussing Francine's problem. Do the children think that she will be able to work out what Queen Smelliefetti looked like, using paintings of her relatives? Ask them to give reasons for their answers, encouraging them to share stories about the ways in which they're similar to their parents/ brothers/sisters or grandparents.

● *We often hear that we're 'just like so-and-so', but how many of us really do look like our parents?* Let's find out, with a game of 'Whose Baby?'

● Encourage the children to take it in turns to examine the photographs and write on the display paper whose relative they think each one is.

● When everyone has had their go, reveal who is who by placing the photograph of the appropriate child next to the photograph of their parent/relative. How many children guessed correctly?

Obtaining evidence

● In science, to prove a theory we need **empirical** evidence.

● We have just seen from the evidence of the family photographs how some of us do indeed look like our parents/relatives. But we don't share all of our traits with them. We may have dad's nose or mum's hair, or we may look more like gran. That's because some traits are more dominant than others. They're more likely to be passed on.

● Using the completed photocopiable sheets, help the children to draw up a series of charts, graphs and data sets to show:
(a) how many members of the class have the same colour hair as one/both of their parents/relatives;
(b) how many members of the class have the same colour eyes as one/both of their parents/relatives;
(c) how many members of the class can curl their tongue/wiggle their ears, and so on;
(d) how many share one of these traits with one or both of their parents/relatives;
(e) how many share all of their traits with one or both of their parents/relatives.

Drawing together

● Summarise the group's findings and help the children to consider what the facts revealed in our surveys tell us.
Can we make any definite statements? For example, 50 per cent of the class have the same colour hair as both parents.

● Some physical traits are recessive others are dominant. *Can we guess from our data which might be which?*
Was Francine right? Do we always look like our parents?

Page
11

Support

Use the photographs and completed photocopiable sheets as inspiration for a piece of non-fiction writing on the theme of 'Why I'm just like my mum/dad'.

Extension

Create photographic family trees.

Scientific language

cells - the smallest part of a living being
genes - chemical instructions which influence how we look
empirical - evidence based on experimentation and observation

Stoking the engine

Setting the context

Thud, thud, thud, thud. "Well I don't know," said Francine, folding the stethoscope away and looking anxiously at Igor. One of her New Year's resolutions had been to take more exercise. Yet after running up and down the stairs of Castle Clutz for 20 minutes, not only was she hot and rosy-cheeked, but her heart was making all sorts of strange noises.

Five minutes later, the stethoscope seemed to prove her worst fears. Her heart beat was definitely much slower now. She also felt cooler and more relaxed. There was no doubt about it - exercise must be bad for you. Or was there some other explanation?

The problem

How can you prove that when you work harder, your heart works harder?

Objectives

To learn that the heart acts as a pump to circulate blood.
To understand the effect of exercise and rest on pulse rate.
To make links between exercise and good health.
To know how a poor diet, alcohol, tobacco and other drugs relate to health.

Background information

Our heart is a hollow muscle, the size of a grapefruit. Heart beats are the motion of the heart **contracting** to pump blood around our bodies. Deoxygenated blood enters the right side of the heart, where it's pumped to the lungs to pick up oxygen. Oxygenated blood returns to the left side of the heart from where it's pumped around our body. Veins always carry blood to the heart. Arteries carry blood away. Valves ensure that blood only travels one way through this **circulatory system**. Exercise makes the heart (like all muscles) bigger and stronger. So 20 minutes of exercise a day for 12 weeks should improve a child's 'heart health' by

between 7 and 26 per cent.

You will need

Space to exercise safely; stethoscope (optional); diagrams/3D model of the heart (optional); photocopiable page 22 (optional).

Per group: stopwatch/clock with second hand; PE shoes.

Discussion and research

● Play '20 Questions'. *Can you guess which part of the body I'm thinking of?* Depending on the age of the group, you may want to refer to an unlabelled model or diagram of the heart as you answer their questions. Use the quiz to introduce facts such as: blood enters and leaves the heart; the differences between these two types of blood; the role of the heart in keeping blood circulating and the fact that the heart is a muscle.
● At the end of the quiz, ask the children to locate their heart.
● When we move our arms and legs, we can feel the muscles working. The beat we feel in our chest is our heart muscle working too;

contracting to pump blood around our body.

Obtaining evidence

● How can we prove to Francine that her heart is meant to beat faster and work harder when she exercises?

● Begin by asking if the children agree, given what they discovered during '20 Questions'?

● Encourage them to suggest ways to test the problem, guiding them towards a comparison of the heart at rest and at work:

    6-8 years - 70-115 bpm (beats per minute)
    9-11 years - 60-110 bpm
    12-16 years - 60-110 bpm
    16+ years - 60-100 bpm
    Athletes - 40-60 bpm

● Measurements of the heart rate at rest should be taken after ten minutes of inactivity. The most commonly used method is to place the second and index finger firmly on the wrist, just under the thumb. (Never use the thumb as this has a pulse of its own.) Multiply the number of beats in 20 seconds by three to find the number of beats per minute.

● Children will need a friend to time them and tell them when to start and stop counting.

● Help the children compare bpm at rest with bpm immediately after five minutes of exercise.

● Then, come together as a class to draw up two comparative graphs, showing bpm at rest and after exercise, for the whole group.

● Other areas for investigation include: Recovery rate: the faster our bpm returns to normal after exercise, the fitter we are. Cardiac Output (CO): the amount of blood pumped by the heart every minute. To calculate, multiply Stroke Rate (SR) by bpm. SR is the amount of blood moved per contraction (beat). 70ml is average for adults. There's no accepted average for children, but 50ml is a median. Divide CO by 1000 to find litres per minute.

Drawing together

● Encourage children to share their findings. *Does the heart work harder when we do? How do we know? Why do some people have lower bpm than others?* (Age, health and fitness are all factors.)

● If our heart is a muscle, speculate what effect regular exercise will have on it.

● Round up by encouraging the children to draw up lists of '20 things we didn't know about the heart'.

Support

Help the children listen to their heart with a stethoscope, if available, and draw up a list of things that are good and bad for the heart. (Emphasise that alcohol, smoking and drugs are as bad as a poor diet and no exercise.)

Extension

Work with the children to make the model of the heart on the photocopiable sheet, exploring blood flow and the effect of valves.

Scientific language

contracting - make smaller
circulatory system - network of arteries and veins which carry blood

Potent potions

Setting the context

Down in the dust-laden laboratory of Castle Clutz, Francine Stein is brewing up a powerful potion. "This is it!" she declared. "At last, this is the invention that will make us rich! No child will ever have to worry about cavities or bad breath again!" Unfortunately, her faithful assistant Igor was being less than helpful. What she really needed was someone to help her test her potion, but while Igor was very faithful, fluffy and fun, he was - after all - only a dog.

The problem

Will Francine's Potion X help protect our teeth from decay?

Objectives

To learn about the functions and care of teeth.
To make links between exercise, a good diet and healthy growth.
To describe changes that occur when materials are mixed.
To know about reversible changes, including dissolving, melting, boiling and freezing.

Background information

The outer layers of our teeth contain minerals that can be dissolved by acidic foods to create cavities. (Sugar feeds the **bacteria** in our mouths to produce more acid.) In the experiment eggs are used because their shells are rich in minerals, although they're not made of the same substance as teeth. Eggs soaked in vinegar become soft as acetic acid breaks apart the calcium carbonate molecules in the shell. The carbon from the carbonate joins with oxygen to make carbon dioxide (the bubbles you seerising from the vinegar). Eggs soaked in cola soften and discolour. Those in coffee also discolour. This can be cleaned off with toothpaste and a brush. Eggs pre-soaked in mouthwash should resist the softening effects, but may still discolour.

You will need

Per group: one Potion X egg; one ordinary hard-boiled egg; two plastic beakers, vinegar, cola and coffee; mouthwash; marker pen; measuring equipment; children's toothbrushes and toothpaste from home (optional); photocopiable page 23.

Preparation

Prepare a batch of exotic-looking bottled 'potions'. Potion X (mouthwash) plus three others containing coffee, cola and vinegar. Hard-boil some eggs. Leave half of the eggs in the mouthwash overnight. Mark these with an X.

Safety Remind children of the importance of never touching or drinking unknown substances.

Discussion and research

● Begin by discussing tooth hygiene.
● As a class, make two lists: one of things that are good for teeth and one of things that are bad.
● Draw out good points such as healthy eating, brushing, flossing, using mouthwash and visiting the dentist. Encourage the children to discuss why these things are good.
● Hand out copies of the photocopiable sheet for the children to complete. This should help them to understand the importance of all of our teeth because they

do different jobs.

● Hand around a glass of Potion X. Ask children to note down its properties (colour, smell, thickness, etc.) and speculate on what it might be. Remind the children not to touch or drink unknown substances.

● Francine thinks that she has the perfect solution to tooth decay: miraculous Potion X. *Is it possible that Potion X can protect teeth from decay?*

Obtaining evidence

● To test how well Potion X works, Francine has worked out a series of experiments to see how it copes with everyday 'nasties' like strong coffee, sugary drinks and the acids in our mouths that cause decay (represented by vinegar).

● Split the children into small Product Development Teams and let each group choose which 'nasty' they want to test.

● Teams should each have two hard-boiled eggs. They may want to measure and weigh each egg before the experiment begins.

● Place both eggs in their own container and cover with the chosen liquid. Mark the level of the liquid on the side of each container. Note the time the experiment began and any **reaction** as the eggs are added. Leave both eggs overnight.

● The following day, note any changes. Consider: *Are the liquids in the jars at the same levels as before? If not, where has it gone? Are the eggs the same as they were before? If not, how have they changed?* (Note their weight, size, appearance and texture.) *Are these changes permanent?*

Drawing together

● Ask the Development Teams to prepare a presentation, using flip charts, whiteboards or PowerPoint to explain what they did and their findings. *Did the eggs soaked in Potion X react in the same way as the untreated eggs?*
Is this what they expected?

● Round up by encouraging children to draw conclusions based on their experiments: *What effects do sugar and acid have on teeth? What might Potion X be?*

Support

As a fun follow-up, use disclosing tablets to test how well toothpaste and mouthwash work on real teeth. After the children have chewed a tablet, take photographs of the results using a digital camera. Help them brush thoroughly, then take another photograph. The next day, ask children to brush and use mouthwash first, then chew a disclosing tablet. Take more photographs and compare the results in a montage.

Extension

Investigate how acidity in the mouth changes after eating different foods. Use litmus paper to test the pH of the mouth before and after each mouthful. (Gargle with water between each test.) As more acid means more decay, discuss with the children the implications of what they've discovered.

Scientific language

bacteria - tiny life forms which usually cause disease
reaction - an effect produced during an experiment

'Dem bones

Setting the context

There's no doubt about it, decided Francine, Cousin Rattle really was looking a little worse for wear. Of course, Igor did keep burying bits of him in the garden, so it really wasn't that surprising. The old medical skeleton had been given to her by her real cousin last Christmas and since then, her dog Igor, kept making off with the juiciest-looking bones. Unfortunately she's been asked to give a talk about 'Our Super Strong Skeleton' at the Clutzberg Institute next week, and the bone that she thinks is the longest and strongest, the femur, seems to be missing. Can you help?

The problem
Is the femur the strongest and longest bone in our skeleton?

Objectives

To learn that humans and some animals have skeletons and muscles to support them, to protect them and to help their bodies move. To make links between exercise, a good diet, and healthy growth.

Background information

Adults have 206 bones. Babies have about 275: some fuse together as we grow. Our bones all have a specific job to do. Some, like the spine, give our body its shape. Others (working together with our muscles) allow us move. Some, like our skull and ribs, protect our organs. The femur (thigh bone) is the longest, heaviest bone in the body. Like all 'long bones' it acts like a lever raising and lowering our leg. 'Short bones' are bridges between other bones. 'Flat bones' are often protective. Every month about five percent of our bone, which is alive, is replaced. We need good food and regular exercise to ensure this happens.

You will need

Large sheets of light-weight cardboard; sticky tape; tape measure; selection of weights tied with string so that they can be easily hung from the test 'bones'; display paper; glue; enlarged copies of photocopiable page 24.

Page
16

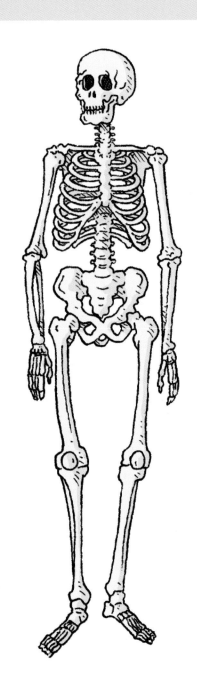

Preparation

Create a display of posters, models and books about the skeleton.

Discussion and research

● Begin with a game of Scientific Simon Says. Ask the children to stand up. The game begins when you name one of the bones in the body. Children must point to that bone and then freeze until you name the next one. Any children who are unable to point to the correct place should sit down.

● Depending on the age of your group, you may want to describe rather than name the bones, or use their scientific rather than common names.

● You may like to include: head (skull); neck (top seven bones of vertebrae); back bone/spine (vertebrae); shoulder blade (scapula); rib cage; pelvis; thigh bone (femur); upper arm (humerus); shin bone (tibia and the smaller fibula); lower arm (ulna and radius); wrist bones (eight carpals); hand bones (five metacarpals); finger bones (14 phalanges); ankle (seven tarsals); sole (metatarsals); toes (14 phalanges).

● At the end of the game, consolidate what the children have learned with a short quiz, repeating the information given to them during Scientific Simon Says as questions.

Obtaining evidence

● *Is the femur the longest and strongest bone in our skeleton? How can we tell?*

● Hand out tape measures and ask children to measure their femur, from the hip to the knee. Note down the length and then measure a selection of other bones for comparison.

● Discuss the children's findings. *How does the length of the femur compare to that of other bones? The femur seems to be the longest bone but is it the strongest?*

● Help the children to make a life-sized model of the femur to test.

● Each child should measure out a cardboard square, the length of their femur. Then roll it tightly and tape it together to make a sturdy 3D model. Explain that bones aren't really solid but in science it is acceptable to use **models** as simplified versions of the real thing.

● Test the model's strength by seeing how much weight it can bear before buckling.

● Make 3D models of other bones and test how strong they are. You may like to allot specific bones to groups of children to allow for comparison later.

● Encourage the children to record their results carefully and clearly, including diagrams as appropriate.

Drawing together

● Round up by asking the children to think about the length, thickness, strength and shape of the femur. *Why is the femur so long? Why is it so thick? What is its job? How did the femur compare to other bones? Is it really the strongest bone in the skeleton? What other types of bones are there in our skeleton?*

● Finally, hand out enlarged copies of the photocopiable sheet and ask the children to re-assemble Cousin Rattle.

● Mount the completed photocopiable pages for presentation to the Clutzberg Institute, complete with appropriate labels.

Support

Enlarge the photocopiable page and allow the children to rebuild Cousin Rattle in groups.

Extension

Help the children to label their completed photocopiable pages with additional information such as the shape, size or job each bone does. Use a coloured key to highlight long, short and flat bones.

Scientific language

model - simplified version of the real thing, used to help with calculations and experiments

Pump it up!

Setting the context

It's no use, Francine decided. Igor was great fun, but sometimes she needed a real helping hand. Unfortunately, Igor only had paws and assistants cost money, which was why, one windy morning, she set out from Castle Clutz to buy a few very special pieces of equipment. However, when Francine arrived at the Inventors R Us store, she realised that the blueprints for her 'Robo Arm' had been blown out of her pocket. It's to phone a friend. Can you help?

The problem

How do you make a working model of an arm?

Objectives

To learn that humans and some animals have skeletons and muscles to support and protect them and help their bodies move.
To make links between exercise, a good diet and healthy growth.

Background information

There are around 630 muscles in our body: smooth muscles, cardiac muscles that make up the heart, and skeletal muscles that give our body shape and enable us to move. Smooth and cardiac muscles are involuntary: we can't consciously control them. Skeletal muscles are voluntary. Skeletal muscles are attached to bones by 'elastic' tissue called tendons. When we contract a muscle, the tendon is pulled up and moves the bone. Muscles can only pull, so for arms to have a full ange of movement, they must work in pairs. In the model, the **biceps** attached to the **humerus**, pull the arm up, allowing us to lift. The **triceps** attached to the **ulna** and **radius**, pull down, allowing us to push.

You will need

A selection of soft bean bags; some heavy books.

Per pair: piece of thin cardboard, sticky tape, string, two balloons, ruler, sharp pencil, scissors; string, bicycle pump (optional).

Preparation

It may be necessary to prepare certain parts of the Robo Arm prior to the lesson, dependent upon the age and ability of the children.

Discussion and research

● Begin by asking the children to lift and carry the heavy books, then throw the bean bags to one another. Ask them to note, carefully, the way their arms move each time.
● When they lift objects up, can they feel the muscles at the back of their arms working? Which muscles 'work' when they throw or push?
● Discuss the way in which our muscles work with bones to create movement, and the fact that muscles can only pull.

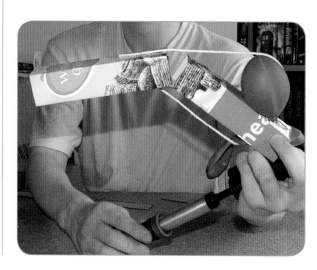

Obtaining evidence

● Demonstrate how to build the Robo Arm:

1. Cut out a sheet of card, 30cm x 15cm. Divide it into five, 3cm - wide columns.
2. Draw a dividing line halfway down the width of the card. Score all lines firmly.
3. Cut the card along the halfway line, leaving just one uncut column in the middle.

4. Fold the card into two, linked, square tubes and tape the edges firmly together.
5. Lie a balloon flat against the top uncut side of the arm. Measure 17cm of string (the ligament). Tape the top of the balloon and string to the tube. Tape the end of the string across the joint.

6. Lie the arm flat and blow up the balloon. You may need a cycle pump.
7. Lie a balloon flat against the top of the cut side of the arm. Measure 25cm of string. Tape the top of the balloon and string to the tube. Tape the end of the string across the joint.
8. Close the arm up and inflate the balloon.

● Label the upper tube 'Humerus', the top of the lower tube 'Radius' and the bottom 'Ulna'. The first balloon represents the biceps, the second the triceps.
● Split the children into pairs and help them choose their equipment.
● Supervise as they make their models. Emphasise the model is not of a complete arm. There are many more muscles, but the biceps and triceps are the most important.

Drawing together

● Ask the children to demonstrate their finished arms. *How successful was the model? What problems did you encounter? How did you solve them? What have we learned about the way muscles work?*
● Finally, help the children to draw up a set of labelled blueprints for the Robo Arm.

Support

Show children how to make the Robo Arm and ask them to design a poster showing the arm's 'life-like qualities'.

Extension

Work together to improve the design.

Scientific language

biceps - muscles at front of upper arm
humerus-long bone between the shoulder and elbow
triceps - muscles at back of upper arm
ulna - forearm bone on side opposite the thumb
radius -forearm bone on the thumb side

It lives... or does it?

- Decide if each of these is living or non-living. Circle the correct word.

cola 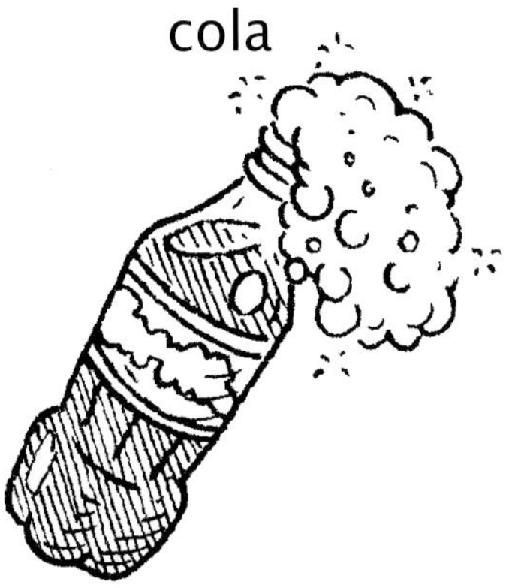 living / non-living	tree 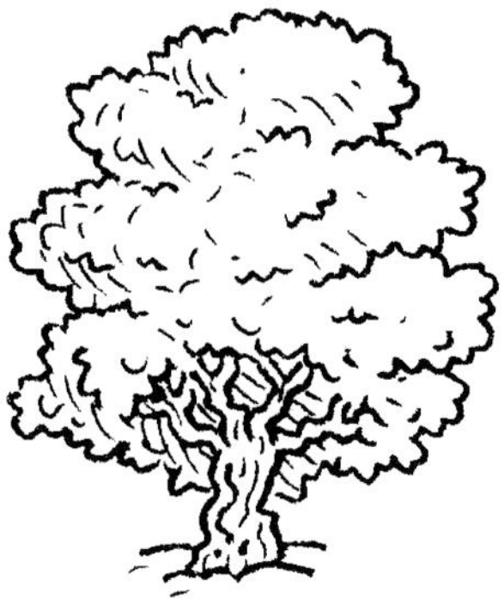 living / non-living	yeast 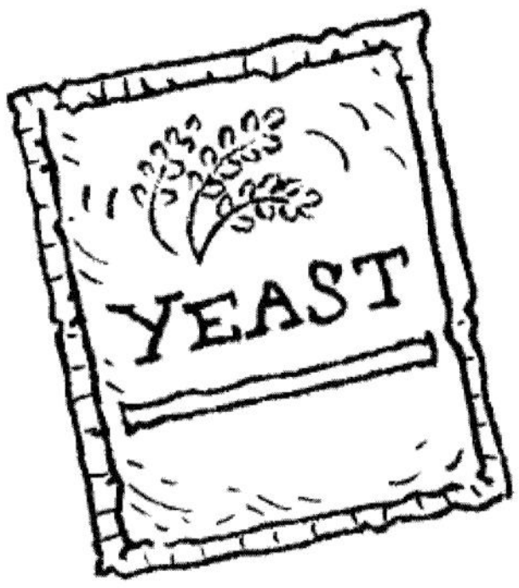 living / non-living
bonfire 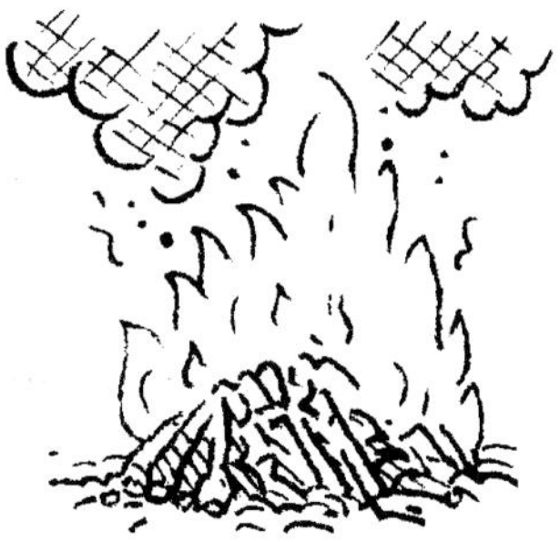 living / non-living	mollusc 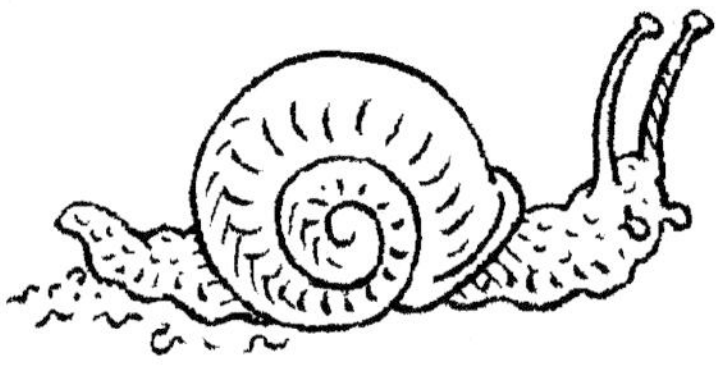 living / non-living	hair 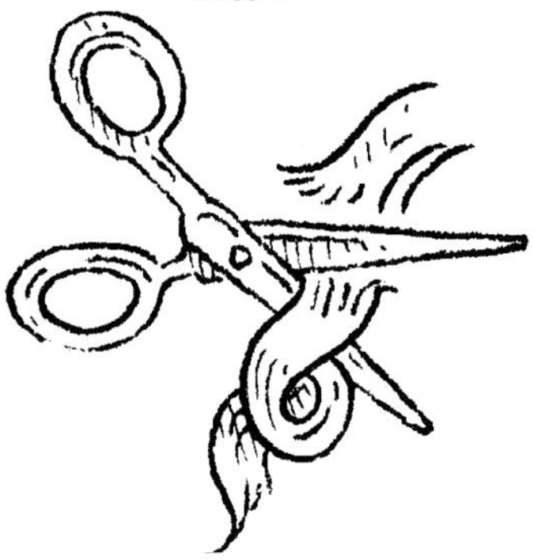 living / non-living
beetle 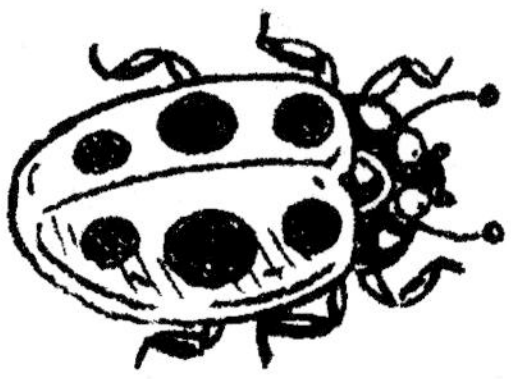 living / non-living	shell 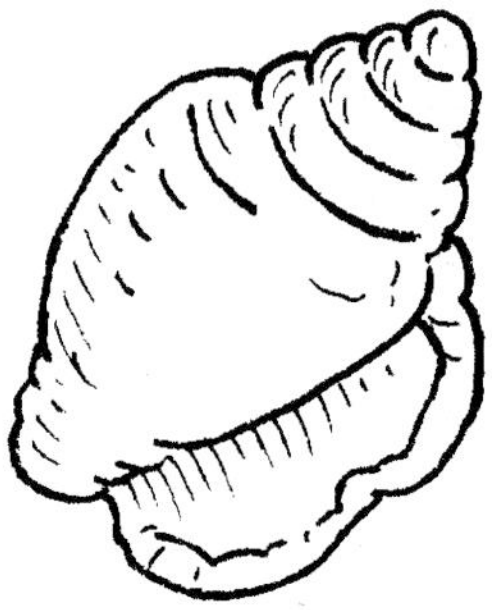 living / non-living	fossil 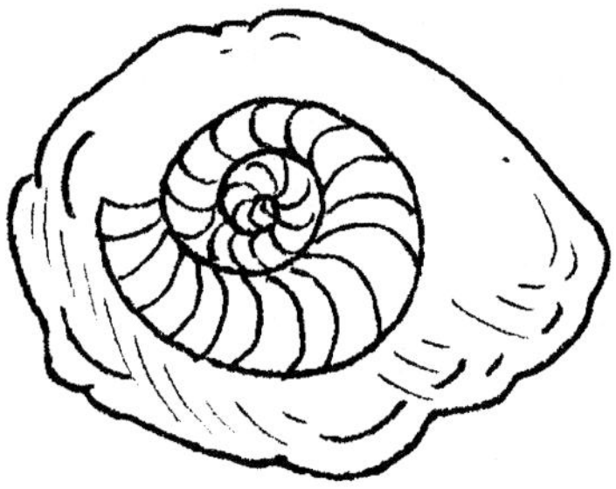 living / non-living

Teacher's notes: This page can be used as a worksheet. Alternatively, enlarge two copies to play living/non-living snap.

Just like Mummy?

Trait	Me		
Tongue curling			
Attached ear lobes			
Short big toe			
Widow's peak			
Hairy fingers			
Do you do this?			
Or this?			
Hair colour			
Eye colour			

Teacher's notes: This sheet can be used for either a class or home survey.

Stoking the engine

● Use these instructions to make your own model of the heart.

a. Label three bottles '**Heart**', '**Blood in**', and '**Blood out**'. ¾ fill 'Blood in' and 'Heart' with water. Add food colouring to 'Blood in'. 	e. Put one straw into 'Heart' bottle–valve first. Make a hole in a spare piece of balloon and push it up the straw and over the bottle to make a lid. Seal with tape.
b. Cut one of your balloons in half widthways. Keep both halves.	f. Put the open end of the straw into 'Blood in'.
c. Take two straws. Split the end of one. Push the ends firmly together to make one long straw.	g. Make another hole in the balloon lid and push the second straw's open end through it. Put the valve end into 'Blood out'.
d. Tape the neck end of a cut balloon over the end of the long straw to make a valve. Repeat steps b, c and d. 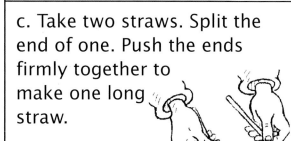	h. Pump the 'Heart' by squeezing the bottle. Keep pumping and watch what happens!

Teacher's notes: You will need: three balloons; four long, bendy straws; sticky tape; three empty plastic bottles; marker pen; food dye; scissors; string; water. Success depends on a good seal over the "Heart" bottle and ensuring the flaps on the valves don't stick together.

■SCHOLASTIC www.scholastic.co.uk

Potent potions

- Cut out and place these teeth in the correct places.

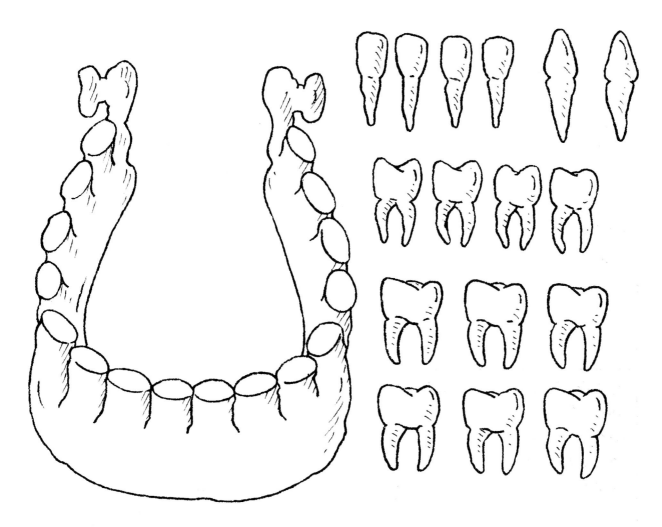

Incisors

These teeth have a sharp, straight, cutting edge.
There are four incisors, all grouped together.

Canines

Canine is another word for a dog; these teeth look like a dog's fangs.
There are two of these sharp, pointed teeth.

Premolars

There are four of these wide, lumpy teeth.
They are made for chewing and crushing food.

Molars

Molars look like premolars, but they are much bigger.
These six teeth are for grinding up food.

'Dem bones

- Rebuild Cousin Rattle!

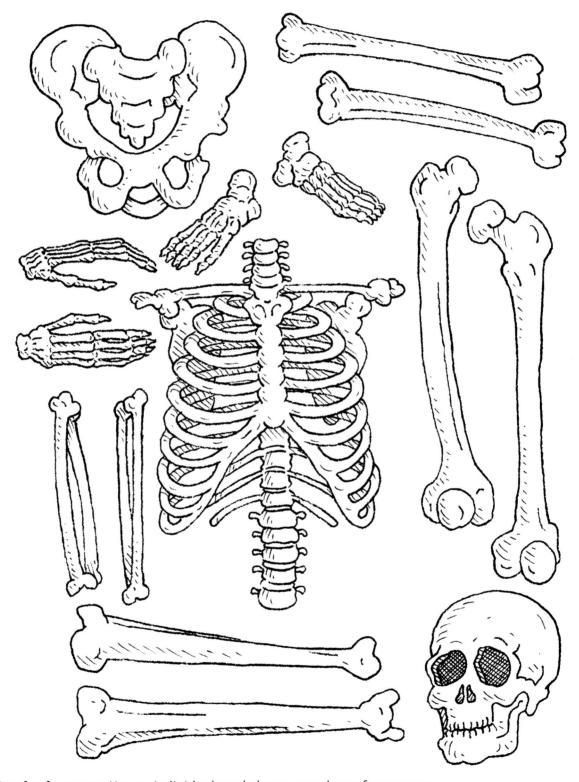

Teacher's notes: Use as individual worksheets or enlarge for groups.

Chapter Two

Our green planet

The six experiments in this chapter are designed to stimulate study through debate, observation and experimentation, and are linked by the theme of 'Life processes and living things'. The activities in this section focus primarily on 'Green plants' and 'Living things in their environment', through introducing and exploring subjects such as plant growth, nutrition, habitat, adaptation, variation, pollution and environmental protection.

● The first activity, **Perfect plants**, encourages children to create their own mini eco-domes in which to test the ideal conditions for growing plants. This activity also takes the opportunity to introduce the idea that, in science, there are often many variables that can affect the results of an experiment - a theme that we return to throughout this chapter. At the end of the activity, children are asked to take on the role of experts on the *TV show Plant an Idea* to present their findings.

● **Root and stem**, **Looking at leaves** and **Amazing algae** are traditional 'test and observe' style experiments. The first stimulates children to discover how water and nutrients are carried, though root and stem, to provide food for the plant. This short experiment is particularly suitable for younger children. The second, long experiment uses basic chemistry to show how a plant's food-making factory shuts down during the autumn. The third deals with algae and introduces the topic of 'Micro-organisms'. Children are encouraged to use their knowledge about plants and animals to determine if algae is alive, and to consider why it's attracted to sunlight.

● **Home sweet home** and **Nature's garden** are two linked activities. The theme of both is habitats and habitat protection. In **Home sweet home** children are taken on a field trip and asked to make their own local Green Guides. **Nature's garden** follows on from this, allowing children to use what they learned about how plants and animals function to design a nature-friendly garden.

● Five photocopiable pages provide follow up, support and extension activities. These include posters for classroom display, card games for younger children, plus record sheets and maps.

Perfect plants

Setting the context

Eco-warrior Errol, is on a mission: to save our planet! In fact, over the years, his eco-friendly campaigns have made him quite famous. So famous, that the Discover! Channel has asked him to appear as an expert guest on their prime-time show *'Plant an Idea'*. They're hoping that Errol will be able to tell their viewers the secrets of growing healthy plants. Unfortunately, Errol is planning to spend the weekend in a bath of cold custard to raise funds to build a nature garden. It looks like he needs a stand in....

The problem

What do plants need to grow and stay healthy?

Objectives

To understand the effects of light, air and water on plant growth.
To know that all living things grow, eat, reproduce and respond to their surroundings.
To make links between living things and the environment in which they are found.

Background information

Green plants need light, water and oxygen to grow. **Germination** can occur in the dark because seeds contain their own limited food supply. Once used up, plants manufacture food through photosynthesis and respiration. Photosynthesis uses the green pigment, chlorophyll, to absorb sunlight. The energy from sunlight is used to split water into its constituent parts. Hydrogen combines with carbon dioxide in air to make a sugar that the plant uses as fuel. Oxygen is a by-product. Respiration doesn't need light. As the sugar is broken down, other by-products combine with oxygen, releasing carbon dioxide and water. Seeds in a dome with wire wool won't grow because they can't respire. Rusting metal 'uses up' the oxygen in the air.

You will need

Video camera and playback facilities (optional); photocopiable page 38.
Per group: mustard/cress seeds (peanut bush kits make a fun alternative); cotton wool; sheet of card; plastic coffee cup 'dome lids' (or the rounded end cut from the bottom of a 2-litre plastic bottle); sticky tape; wire wool; disposable gloves; marker pen.
Safety Gloves are advisable when handling wire wool as it may irritate skin.

Preparation

Create a display of various types of fruit and seeds, including apples, cut open to reveal the seeds inside and coconuts.

Discussion and research

● Begin by handing around a selection of seeds. Encourage the children to discuss them, commenting on what they see, feel and smell. *What do all of these items have in common? How are they different? What do seeds like these need to grow?*
● During the discussion, draw out how seeds are living things that need water and

air (containing oxygen) to grow. Light is only necessary once the nutrients in the seed cases have been used up.

● Before we can take Errol's place on *Plant an Idea*, we need to know a little more about what plants need to grow. We can do this by growing our own plants.

Obtaining evidence

● Demonstrate how to make a basic 'eco-dome':

1. The damp cotton wool needs to be stretched out, flattened, and sprinkled with seeds.

2. Place the cotton wool on the square of card and cover with a dome.

3. Stick the dome down onto the card. If you're using coffee cup lids, you'll also need to tape up the drinking holes. Explain that the reason for this is to give us an environment that we can control, which is important in science.

4. Label each experiment clearly with a marker pen. Note the start time/date and agree with the children when you will end the experiment. (Seeds should grow within 2-6 days, depending on conditions.)

● Split the group into Discovery Teams to explore how the seeds react to one or more of the following **variables**:

Wet cotton wool, placed in a sunny spot.

Dry cotton wool, placed in a sunny spot.

Wet cotton wool, placed in a dark drawer/ cupboard.

Dry cotton wool, placed in a dark drawer/ cupboard.

Wet cotton wool, placed in a sunny spot. Add wire wool.

Dry cotton wool, placed in a sunny spot. Add wire wool.

Wet cotton wool, placed in a dark drawer/ cupboard. Add wire wool.

Dry cotton wool, placed in a dark drawer/ cupboard. Add wire wool.

● Alternatively, work with the children to draw up a list of their own variables.

Drawing together

● Round up the experiments by drawing up a table to show the group's results. Give the

Photo © Stock.xchng.

experiment a tick if the seeds were given light, oxygen and water. *How many ticks were needed for the seeds to grow? Did the seeds in the dark grow as well as those in the light?* Discuss what our results tell us before helping the children to present their findings on *Plant an Idea*.

● Depending on the age/confidence of the children, either take on the role of the presenter/interviewer, calling on expert witnesses from each group, or help them devise their own presentation, complete with visual aids. (This can be recorded if you have suitable equipment.)

Support

Hand out copies of the photocopiable sheet for the children to complete.

Extension

Explore how well seeds, supplied with water and air, grow in sunlight compared to artificial light.

Scientific language

germination - when plants start to grow

variable - something that can be changed

Root and stem

Setting the context

When Errol isn't helping save the Earth, he helps his friends, Josh, Jake and Jeannie, run the Green Scene Cafe. Their speciality is Surprise Salad: orange onions, blue radishes
and red celery! Josh can never figure out how Errol manages to grow such odd coloured vegetables but, according to Errol, the secret is in understanding how plants 'work'.

"The really neat thing about plants," he explained "is that their four main parts work together to make food. Just like the four of us." Josh looked baffled. "Here," said Errol, giving Josh one of his wide, wide smiles, "let me show you."

The problem

How do plants make food?

Objectives

To learn about the part played by leaves in helping plants grow.
To know how roots anchor plants in place and help them take in water and minerals.
To understand the effects of light, air and water on plant growth.

Background information

A plant's life starts when primary roots push through the seed's outer coating. While the root grows down, the stem pushes up, towards the light. Once through the soil's surface, leaves and flowers begin to sprout. Growing plants have four important parts: roots, stem, leaves and flowers. Roots take up water and minerals from the soil. These are carried along the stem to tiny 'veins' in the leaves. We can see this in action when we dye the celery. Green leaves help convert light and water into food through **photosynthesis**. Flowers and fruit provide seeds, so the whole process can begin again.

You will need

Per group: plastic beaker; piece of celery with leaves (or white flowers, such as carnations); water; food colouring; spoon; marker pen.

Preparation

Prepare an A3, laminated copy of

photocopiable page 39. Cut out each of the labels and fix double-sided sticky tape to the back.

Discussion and research

● Begin by showing the children the enlarged copy of the photocopiable sheet. Together, discuss the diagram and share any knowledge the children have of how plants grow and develop. If appropriate, remind them of previous experiments relating to how plants grow.

● Ask for volunteers to place the sticky labels, one at a time, in the correct place on the diagram. Encourage the children to explain their reasons for the positioning of each label. Then, remind them of Josh's problem.

● From what they know about how plants make food, and from what they can see on the diagram, can they suggest how Errol might create his Surprise Salad?

● Note down the children's ideas before drawing out any appropriate suggestions.

Obtaining evidence

● Split the children into groups. Help each group to set up and carry out their experiment:

1. Fill the jar, half-full with cold water. Mark the level of the water carefully.

2. Add enough food dye to produce a rich colour, and stir well.

3. Place the thickest part of the celery in the water.

4. Place the celery on a window sill and observe.

5. After an agreed time, remove the celery from the water.

● It should take at least two hours to begin to see the dye as it travels up the stem of the celery.

● The top end of the celery and leaves will show the dye first. More detail can be seen if sections are cut open. Leave overnight for more dramatic results.

● Before the children begin, allow them to suggest ways of making sure that everyone's experiment is as accurate as possible. For example, *how much water should you use? Does the size of the celery stick matter? How*

long should the celery be left in the water? What about the amount of dye you add? Will its colour make a difference to your results? How can all of these things be measured accurately?

● After the activity, encourage any children whose experiments were not successful to try again, asking other groups for advice if appropriate.

Drawing together

● Ask children to consider what the coloured celery tells them about how plants take in water and minerals from the soil. *What equipment did we use? How did we set up our experiment? What happened to the level of the water in the jar? Why did the celery change colour? How are these two things linked? What does this have to do with how plants make food?*

● *What else do you notice?* Encourage the children to look at the leaves carefully.

● Finally, challenge the children to write up their own 'Recipe for Surprise Salad', including step-by-step diagrams/digital photographs, plus any measurements and instructions.

Support
As a follow up, work with the children to create a menu for the Green Scene Cafe. Include as many edible plants as possible.

Extension
Repeat the experiment to compare the internal 'food highways' of a wide range of plants and vegetables. Spring onions and leeks work well. These will also put out roots within a few days, and this can be interesting for children to observe.

Scientific language
photosynthesis - when green plants use light and water to make food

Looking at leaves

Setting the context

East Enderling Environmental Committee is worried. They've been carrying out a survey of plants and have discovered some disturbing 'facts'. Not only have the plants' leaves changed colour, but the plants themselves appear to have stopped growing. Errol has tried to reassure them that this is quite natural: the leaves change colour because the plants' growth slows. Unfortunately, the Committee isn't convinced by his arguments. "We know that leaves always change colour in the autumn," they said, "but what has that got to do with how fast or slow the plants grow?"

The problem

Is there a link between leaves changing colour in the autumn and the plants' slower growth rate?

Objectives

To learn about the part played by leaves in helping plants grow.
To know how roots anchor plants in place and help them take in water and minerals.
To be able to name the parts of a flower and understand its role in helping plants reproduce.
To understand the effects of light, air and water on plant growth.

Background information

Photosynthesis occurs inside fully grown leaves. The process creates food, enabling plants to grow. Photosynthesis relies on a green **pigment** in leaves, called chlorophyll. In autumn, there isn't enough light for photosynthesis, so plants 'shut down'. When this happens, chlorophyll starts to fade, revealing yellow and red pigments that were in the leaves already, but were covered by the chlorophyll. This experiment uses chromatography to separate and compare the amount of 'food-making' chlorophyll in green and autumnal leaves. The less chlorophyll, the less a plant will grow. Other pigments present in leaves include carotenoids (yellow) and anthocyanins (red/purple). Both pigments create an orange colour.

You will need

Water; kettle.

Per group: one beaker per test; a selection of large leaves of varying colours (at least three of each colour per child/group); scissors; spoon/mortar and pestle; surgical spirit; boiling water; one blotting paper strip per test; tin foil or jar lid; baking tray; digital camera and print out facilities (optional); photocopiable page 40.

Safety Seek immediate medical help should surgical spirit be taken internally.
Boiling water and steam can burn; supervise children closely.

Preparation

Cut the blotting paper into long, thin strips. Prepare several tests at different stages to speed up the explanation of the process during the lesson (optional).

Discussion and research

● Begin by handing round a selection of leaves. Discuss their shape, size, texture and colours.
● Ask children to think about what Errol said. *Do you think it's true? Why?*
● *How can we tell that the colour change is because the plant has stopped growing rather than just a natural, seasonal event?*
● Explain that we can test for chlorophyll. If Errol is right, then autumnal plants should have less chlorophyll because plants don't need to make food when they stop growing.

Obtaining evidence

● Ideally each child/group should test at least two leaves - one dark green, and one containing more 'autumnal' colours. (Use a digital camera to take photographs of the leaves. These can be mounted beside the finished chromatogram.)
● As with all experiments there are many possible variables. Discuss with the children ways of standardising their experiments, by ensuring that the leaves are all a similar size, shape and hue, by measuring the amount of surgical spirit used and by agreeing a length of time to leave the solution and blotting strips.
● Demonstrate the experiment. (You may like to use your pre-prepared tests to save time.):
1. Cut up your leaf and grind it in a mortar or mash with a spoon. This helps release the chemicals stored in the leaves.
2. Put the ground leaf in a jar. Add enough surgical spirit to cover. Stir well.
3. Wash and dry the scissors,mortar and spoon.
Repeat the process for additional leaves.
4. Stand the jar(s) in a baking tray of boiling water. Loosely rest the lids on the top of the jars. Hot water acts as a **catalyst** and should be replaced as soon as it starts to cool.
5. Wait until the surgical spirit is a good, dark colour. The time this takes depends on the type of leaves, their colour, and how well they were 'mashed'.
6. Place one end of a strip of blotting paper in each solution. As the surgical spirit evaporates, pigments will be pulled up the paper - the smallest amounts of pigment tend to move the furthest up the paper.
7. Leave for at least two hours, until the colours fully separate. For best results, leave for the whole day.
8. Allow the blotting paper(s) to dry thoroughly before analysing.

Drawing together

● *What pigment do green leaves contain? What is the job of this pigment? Do leaves really change colour in the winter? In our experiments which leaves - apart from green - contained the most green pigment? What do these colour changes have to do with the changing seasons? Was Errol right? Why?*
● Finally, write a letter to the East Enderling Environmental Committee, explaining how plant growth affects leaf colour.

Support

Make a scrap book of leaves of different colours and shapes. Include broad, narrow (like grass) and needle-shaped leaves.

Extension

Support the children in completing the photocopiable sheet. How many pigments can they identify?

Scientific language

pigment - a natural substance which gives colour to plants or animals
catalyst - something which increases the speed of a chemical reaction

Amazing algae

Setting the context

Errol's on a pollution-busting campaign. He's been testing the purity of the water in the local lake. Unfortunately, there seems to be something wrong with his samples. When he returned home, he put one in a dark cupboard for safe keeping. There wasn't room in the cupboard for the other sample, so he left it on the window sill but now the water has turned green. Errol thinks this could be really serious. What's causing it? Could it be natural? What he needs is someone to help him test his ideas....

The problem

What's making the water turn green?

Photo © Stock.xchng.

Objectives

To understand that micro-organisms exist, even though they are often too small to be seen.
To make links between living things and the environment in which they are found.
To know that all living things grow, eat, reproduce and respond to their surroundings.

Background information

Living things are made up of tiny cells. Humans contain around 50 trillion cells, but some living things contain just one. These single-celled life-forms are usually so small they can only be seen under a microscope. The blue-green algae, found in water, is a type of single-cell bacteria. Colonies of algae gather on the surface of water, where there's lots of sunlight. There they photosynthesise, like plants. Pollution can destroy the **ecological balance** of a lake, allowing algae to grow out of control. These algal blooms poison the water. However, in small amounts, algae provides food for the fish and oxygenates the water.

You will need

Hot water/antiseptic wipes to clean hands after the experiment; DVD of *George Shrinks*, *Fantastic Voyage*, *Honey I Shrunk the Kids* (or something with a similar theme).

Per group: one jam jar containing the pre-prepared water mix; heavy-weight parcel tape; scissors.

Safety Stagnant water can cause serious illnesses. Children should not touch/drink the water. Hands should be washed thoroughly after the experiment. Reinforce the message that children should never go near any body of water unattended.

Preparation

Just before the activity, collect some 'green' water. (Wear protective gloves when you do this.) Mix 30:70, with tap water and stir so that the algae is dispersed. Divide the water between enough jam jars for the whole class. Seal the lids tightly and keep the jars in a dark place.

Discussion and research

● If you have the facilities, show a scene from *George Shrinks*, *Fantastic Voyage* or *Honey I Shrunk the Kids*. We can't really miniaturise ourselves, but if we could then what sort of strange world would we see? The film may be fiction, but there are lots of things that live in our world that are too small to see without a microscope.

● *Could there be some **microscopic** life in the water which makes it turn green? If so, why did only one of the jars of water turn green? Perhaps it's some type of pollution or pigment?*

● Inspire the group to share their ideas before taking a vote on what they think is the most likely explanation.

Obtaining evidence

● In science, often the best way to understand a problem is to recreate it. However, if we copy what Errol did exactly then we still won't understand why only one of the jars of water turned green.

● We need to test the same water under both conditions. Can the children think of ways this could be possible?

● Some children may want to repeat what Errol did - placing one jar, first in the cupboard, then on the window sill, to compare results. Challenge the children to

decide which test they want to do first. Does the order matter? Perhaps some groups could try the test one way, and some the other?

● Alternatively, a more dramatic demonstration is to cover the jar in heavy parcel tape, leaving just one square of glass on the side uncovered. Then, place the jar in sunlight.

● Timing and results will vary depending on how much algae was in the water originally, but after a few hours, the algae in the jar should have started to gather around the uncovered area of glass. This can be clearly seen when the parcel tape is removed.

Drawing together

● Remind the children about the work they did to determine whether something is 'living' or 'non-living' (see pages 8-9). *Could the 'green stuff' be alive? What clues do we have from its behaviour? Why might it need sunlight?*

● Work together to decide what made the water turn green. *What 'clues' do we have? Is it alive? Is it a plant or an animal? Why can't we see it?*

Support

Water containing algae can make us ill. Round up work with the children by stimulating them to design their own safety posters on the theme of 'Green for Danger'.

Extension

Encourage the children to write up a report, in the style of a science journal, detailing their findings.

Scientific language

ecological balance - when living things and their environment live in harmony
microscopic - something that cannot be seen without a microscope

Home sweet home

Setting the context

East Enderling Environmental Committee has decided that the town's latest shopping centre needs a big, new car park. So they've decided to build one on a local field. "It's big, it's ugly and no one is using it," they said in a recent announcement to the Press. However, Errol isn't very happy about their decision. "This field might not look very attractive because it looks messy, wild and overgrown to us," he said in reply, "but it's an important habitat for plants and animals. To them it's home."

The problem

How can you find out if the local area provides an important habitat for plants and animals?

Photo © Stock.xchng.

Objectives

To consider the ways in which living things and the environment need our protection.
To identify and group local plants and animals.
To know that different plants and animals are found in different habitats.
To use maps and keys to share information.

Background information

In the past, scientists used Greek or Latin as a common language. That's why **habitat** comes from a Latin word meaning 'it inhabits'. When environmentalists talk about habitats they mean the physical environments in which flora (plant) and fauna (animal) species live. The types of habitat available - whether wet, dry, hot or cold - affect what species are present. (The Eden Project domes are really huge, artificial habitats, known as 'biomes'.) Pollution and habitat destruction can cause wide-scale and sudden extinctions because plants and animals tend to adapt to live in certain areas.

You will need

Measuring equipment; magnifying glasses; sample bags/jars; note/sketch books; tracing paper; crayons; digital cameras; photocopiable page 41.

Safety Ensure that children consult you before handling any plants and that they wash their hands thoroughly after the field trip.

Preparation

Choose a suitable area for study. This may be a local park, woodland or school field. Ideally, the 'land for development' shouldn't be too artificial or managed. It should also offer a wide range of different habitats for study. You may need to formally arrange the visit.

Discussion and research

● Begin by explaining that, to help Errol, we are going to compile a 'Field Guide' showing what the land threatened with development is like.

● Discuss with the children what sort of information needs to be in the Guide.

● Together, consider how best to gather the information then and draw up a contents list. You may like to include:

An annotated map.

Some background information about the area. For example, what can we find out about how the land has been used by looking in the library or by interviewing local people?

Sketches/photographs/descriptions of local plants and animals. (Rubbings can also be made using tracing paper and a soft, wax crayon.)

Samples of flowers and leaves. These can be pressed between sheets of blotting paper.

A species reference guide: make a cardboard 'transect' frame, 30cm x 30cm. Place on the ground in various locations and count the number of different species inside each frame. The areas where there are the fewest/greatest variety of species can then be marked on the map.

● Finally, draw up an equipment list. Think about suitable clothing and transportation as well as the scientific equipment.

Obtaining evidence

● On the day of the field trip, split the children into groups. Then, either ask for volunteers or allot different research jobs to each group.

● During the day, help children to keep detailed notes of where different types of plants and animals are found and what their habitats are like: whether it's light, dark, wet, dry, or what the soil is like.

● Remind them that they are not there to destroy the environment! This means that they shouldn't trample the flowers, pull up the plants or disturb the wildlife. Samples should only be taken of fallen leaves/flower heads, blades of grass.

● Throughout the day, encourage children to be thorough. If animals aren't in plain view, try lifting up rocks or checking around tree trunks. Magnifying glasses can be useful.

Drawing together

● Even a small field can be a vibrant habitat for plants and animals. After the trip, consider what has been learned about the types of species found locally. *Were the same species always found in similar areas? What does this suggest? Were you surprised how many different plants and animals you discovered? Why?*

● *Is the area that you studied really a valuable habitat for plants and animals? If not, how could it be improved?* Discuss ideas for attracting more wildlife into the area.

● Finally, as a group, decide how the information can best be presented, before putting together a class 'Field Guide'.

Support

Introduce children to the topic of habitats using the photocopiable sheet.

Extension

Work with the children to draw up posters and flyers for Errol's campaign to help keep local green spaces safe for wildlife.

Scientific language

habitat - natural home of a plant or animal

Nature's garden

Setting the context

Since Errol's campaign to stop East Enderling Environmental Committee building its new car park, there's been a sudden surge of interest in green issues. It seems that everyone's been talking about how they can make a little more space for nature in their lives, which is why Errol has decided to run a competition to get everyone inspired.

The only rules are that the garden designs should be simple, fun for everyone and (most importantly of all) respect existing habitats and wildlife.

The problem

How do you design a nature-friendly garden?

Objectives

To know that different plants and animals are found in different habitats.
To understand the 'web of life' and its importance in maintaining a healthy environment.
To consider the ways in which living things and the environment need our protection.
To identify and group local plants and animals.
To use maps and keys to share information.

Background information

Plants and animals are nature's natural specialists. Over time they are able to **adapt** to local conditions, with the result that almost every corner of our planet, from sun-scorched deserts to tropical rainforests, is teeming with life. If we look around us we'll see that, even in our local area, there are many different types (species) of plants and animals. Each of these depends on the other for its survival, creating a complex **web of life**. Designing a garden that is good for wildlife, depends on respecting and maintaining this delicate balance.

You will need

Sheets of graph paper; tracing paper; tape measures/measuring wheels; rulers; coloured pencils; photocopiable page 42.

Preparation

Ideally children should have access to a safe outdoor space where they can work undisturbed. As this isn't always possible, this activity can be carried out on a purely theoretical basis, in which case, you'll need to prepare a suitable map from which the children should work.

Discussion and research

● Remind the children of the work completed during their field trip (see pages 34-35).
● Explain that they're now going to design their own nature garden, using what they've learned about habitats and 'natural spaces'.
● Begin by helping the children to make a large plan-drawing on graph paper of the site of their proposed nature garden. Include any prominent local features, such as the school.
● Pin up the plan on the wall for future reference.

Obtaining evidence

● Divide the plan into 'plots' and allot a plot to each child/group.

● Hand out graph paper and help the children to make a detailed plan of their existing plot. Mark living features, such as grass or trees on the paper, as well as man-made objects. They may like to design a key to show these.

● They should also make notes on details such as how much light the plot gets, or what the soil is like, as this will affect what can live there. Now ask each group to design their new plot.

● As a starting point, a good design should:
(a) be simple and 'low-maintenance'.
(b) include something of interest all year round. This includes plants that will grow all year (perennials) as well as those which only bloom for a few months (annuals).
(c) be suited to local conditions. From their field trip, what plants do the children know will grow well in the area?
(d) make the best use of the space they have. (So, in a confined space, small shrubs and bushes may be better than trees.)
(e) attract wildlife: think about potential habitats, such as logs and rocks for insects to hide under. Consider food chains: what foods do birds/insects and mammals need?

● They'll need to take into account what they've previously learnt about variation and habitats. For example, it may be fine to 'landscape' a concrete car park, but a field will have its own established wildlife, so their designs shouldn't disturb local plants/animals too much.

● Ask children to draw their proposed designs on the tracing paper, laid over their original plan, so that they can take into account existing features.

● Once the children have decided on their garden design, challenge them to draw, on a fresh sheet of graph paper, their new plan.

Drawing together

● Round up the activities by sticking together completed plans to give a picture of how the finished nature garden will appear.

● Together, discuss the new nature garden and compare it with how the space looked previously.

● Encourage the children to consider and evaluate their work critically. *Which elements work best? What would you change? Would the garden look better if you had worked on the design together, rather than just focusing on your own plots?*

● Finally, vote on which plot should win Errol's competition.

Page 37

Support

Provide the children with a copy of the photocopiable sheet and offer them as much or as little help as they need to complete it.

Extension

As a follow up, stimulate the children to keep their own wildlife diaries. Include information such as the date, place, time, weather and place that the plant/animal was spotted as well as a description/sketch.

Scientific language

adapt - to change to suit new conditions
web of life - the way in which all living things depend on one another

Perfect plants

● Match these seeds with the plants that they will grow into. What are their names?

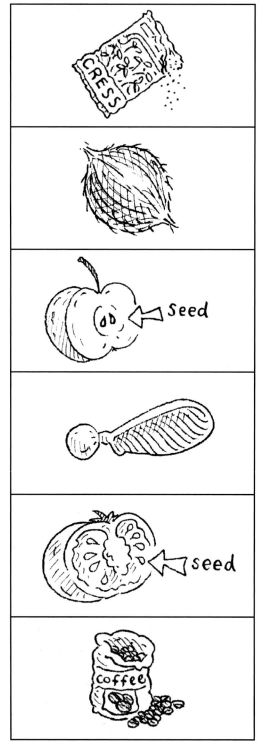

Teacher's notes: This page can be used as a worksheet. Alternatively, enlarged copies can be used as cards for group 'snap'.

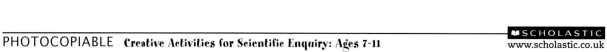

Root and stem

- Label this picture.

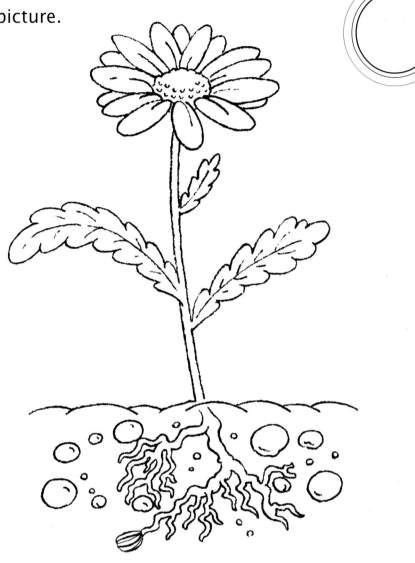

green leaves	flowers	seed
sunlight	stem	roots
soil	oxygen	takes in water and minerals
helps photosynthesis	produces seeds	carries minerals and water

Teacher's notes: This page can be used as a worksheet. Alternatively, enlarge to A3 for display. Cut out and laminate the labels and fix double-sided tape to the back.

Looking at leaves

• Use this sheet to record your work.

[Glue your blotting paper here]

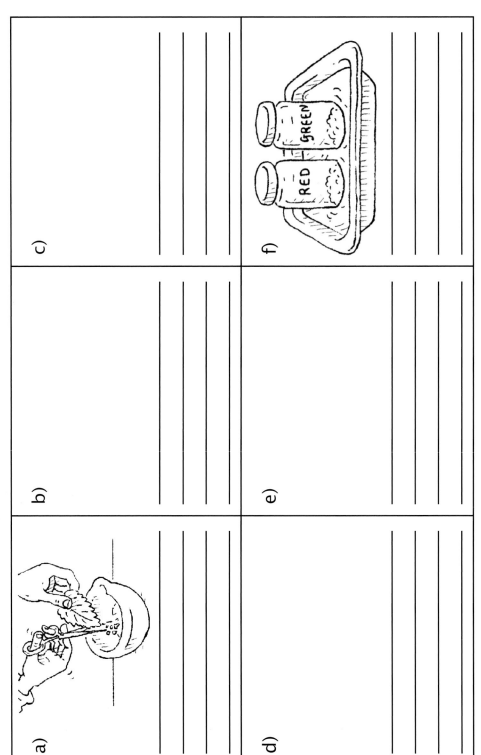

a)

b)

c)

d)

e)

f)

Home sweet home

● Match these animals to their natural habitats.

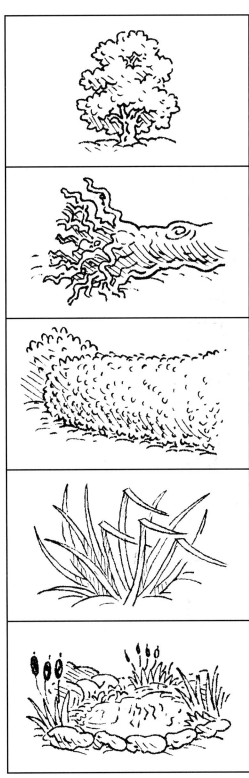

Teacher's notes: This page can be used as an individual worksheet, or enlarged and used with whole groups.

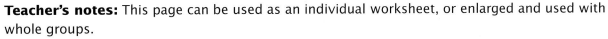

Nature's garden

- Cut out and stick down these pictures to make this garden wildlife friendly.

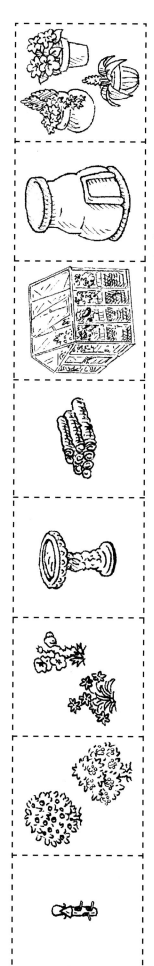

Infinity & beyond

The six activities in this section use the character of Anuska the Astronaut to introduce topics that focus on the themes of 'Materials and their properties' and 'Forces and motion'. The activities include a range of focused and fun tasks including model making, 'test and discover' experiments, data logging and discussion. Although the character of Anuska inhabits a fictional future world of Space School, the science is firmly based on what children can experience for themselves in the real world.

- In **Splash down!** children are stimulated to make, design and test their own space capsules. By comparing and testing the properties of a wide range of everyday materials, children are challenged to get their 'egg-onaut' to the planet's surface in one piece!

- **Create a crater** continues the theme of 'Materials and their properties' by looking at rocks, soils and their characteristics. Children

are encouraged to test each material in turn, by making their own classroom craters.

- **Don't drink the water!** offers a practical demonstration of how some materials change when they are mixed and how these mixed materials can be separated again. The water filter can be made using the same test materials as in **Create a crater**, giving an ideal opportunity to consolidate learning.

- **Roaring rockets** and **Fun with friction** can be used as linked activities. The first uses balloon power to explore the forces that act on a rocket: thrust, fluid friction (drag) and gravity. Children then go on to experiment and make links between the amount of force applied to an object and the distance it moves. The second activity looks in more detail at friction, encouraging children to test out their home-made Space Rovers.

- As our fictional guide through this chapter is an astronaut we finish with an activity based on the topic of 'The Earth and beyond'. **Planet spotting** shows children how to do make their own pinhole viewers. Further experiments that give children the chance to explore our Solar System can be found in **Smile please!** (pages 62-63) and **All in a day's work** (pages 88-89). **Planet spotting** also offers a good introduction to vision and the everyday effects of light.

- Five photocopiable activity sheets are provided at the end of this chapter to further support and extend the children's work.

Roaring rockets

Setting the context

When Anuska was younger she dreamed of travelling into space. Now she's at Space School she gets to spend all day with some of the world's most famous astronauts. Yet what she enjoys most of all is watching the shuttles and rockets being launched. The spectacle of those huge lumps of metal being hurled upwards into the depths of space never fails to amaze her. In fact, as her friend Oleg is graduating next week, Anuska's planning a special party, complete with home-made rockets that work just like the real thing....

The problem

Do Anuska's rockets really work 'just like the real thing'?

Objectives

To identify and measure types of force.
To learn that friction is a type of force which slows moving objects.
To know that gravity pulls objects down towards the Earth.

Background information

Objects only move when a **force**, such as a push or pull, is applied to them. The amount an object moves is always equal to the force applied to it. Other forces, such as **friction** and **gravity**, act to slow movement. Fluid friction (drag) occurs when any solid moves through air or water. (The larger an object, the more friction acts upon it.) Gravity pulls all objects down towards the Earth. So to move a rocket we must generate another force, called 'thrust', by burning exhaust gases. Thrust pushes the rocket upwards. Although we're simplifying the process somewhat, the principles involved in moving rockets and balloons are the same.

You will need

Space to set out a 'launch pad'; images/video of rockets or space shuttles taking off (optional).

Per group: one sausage-shaped balloon; peg; thin cardboard; ball of string; sticky tape; tape measure.

Preparation

Locate images or video of rockets or space shuttles launching. Digg offer spectacular slow motion capture images of rockets taking off on their web site: www.ioindustries.com/flashvideo.htm

Discussion and research

● If possible, use images of rockets being launched and share these with the children.
● Then blow up a balloon and let it go. Challenge the children to make links between the real-life rockets and the balloon.
● Discuss the forces which act on objects in motion, drawing out the concept that the amount an object moves is always equal to the force applied to it. *Do these rules always apply?*

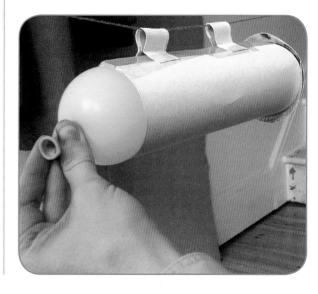

Obtaining evidence

● To prove or disprove Anuska's statement that home-made rockets work 'just like the real thing' we need to test for ourselves.

● Show the children how to make their own rockets:

1. Make a tube out of thin cardboard, 25cm long by 20cm wide.
2. Cut out a cardboard circle, twice the diameter of the end of the tube.

3. Draw a line across the radius of the circle and cut across.
4. Roll the circle into a cone and tape together. Stick the cone to the tube.
5. Cut out two strips of paper, 8cm long by 2cm wide.

6. Roll each strip of paper into a loop and tape to the side of the tube.

● Once the children have made their rockets, set out a launch pad by placing rows of chairs at either end of the room.

● Measure out the string into lengths long enough to stretch between both rows of chairs.

● Tie one end of the string to the back of a chair. Feed the loops on the rocket through the string. Tie the other end of the string to the other chair.

● Repeat for each rocket.

● Blow up the sausage-shaped balloons and fit one into each tube.

● Use a peg to keep the air in the balloon until the rocket trials begin.

● Experiment with different amounts of 'force' (one puff, two puffs, etc.) to see how far each rocket travels.

Drawing together

● Round up by asking children to name three of the forces that affect how their rockets perform. *What does each force 'do'?*

● *Is there a link between the amount of 'fuel' and the distance the rocket travels? Why? Does this mean that big rockets will always travel further than smaller?* (Remind the children that a bigger rocket is also heavier, so is more affected by friction.)

● Finally, decide if Anuska was right. *Although our rockets are only models, how do they compare with the real thing?*

Page
45

Support
As an alternative, hold simple balloon races and measure the distance each balloon travels. Compare the results with how much fuel each balloon was given.

Extension
Experiment with different-sized rockets and smaller/larger balloons.

Scientific language
force - a type of energy which produces a change in the motion of an object
friction - a force created by two objects rolling over each other
gravity - a force which pulls objects towards the centre of a planet or moon

Splash down!

Setting the context

Since winning her place in Space School, Anuska has started to think that she might have made a big mistake. In the last few months she's been spun round and round in a giant centrifuge until she was almost sick. She's spent hours in freezing water learning what it's like to be weightless and now she's having to get to grips with the science of it all. "Oh!" she sighed, frustratedly, "who cares what the capsule is made of?" "Well you might do," laughed her Professor, "if it's made of the wrong things!"

The problem

Why are some materials 'right' for the job and some 'wrong'?

Objectives

To compare everyday materials and objects on the basis of their material properties.

Background information

Traditional spacecrafts contain a Command Module, where the crew live and operate the craft, a Service Module, containing the fuel and engines, and a Lunar Module. A rocket launches the whole craft into space. All parts of a spacecraft need to withstand the extreme temperatures found in space. They must also be light to save fuel (as they have to carry all they need), tough, but flexible enough to be stressed without breaking. The Capsule, designed to protect the Apollo 11 Lunar Module, was made from a 42.5mm thick aluminium honeycombed material. Outside was a 1m layer of **insulating** cork.

You will need

Per group: raw or hard-boiled eggs; a selection of test materials; parcel tape; glue; scissors; photocopiable page 56.

Preparation

Source a wide range of test materials such as cotton wool; tissue paper; aluminium foil; corrugated cardboard; bubble wrap; polystyrene; cardboard tubes; empty cocoa tins. Raw eggs give more dramatic results although they're harder to keep in one piece. (Children can get disappointed if none of their eggs survive the fall.) If using hard-boiled eggs, painting the shells will make it easier to spot hairline cracks. Cut up the egg boxes to make individual 'capsules' for each egg-onaut. As egg boxes are designed to protect the egg, it is also important that you discover, beforehand, exactly what height the egg needs to be dropped from to ensure it breaks.

Discussion and research
● Begin with a simple but dramatic demonstration: dropping a raw egg from height.
● Remind the children about what Anuska said about space capsules. Just imagine if the egg had been Anuska! Now we can see why it's important that the materials from which the capsule and the rest of the vehicle are made have just the right properties.
● We aren't able to test real space materials but we can test to see which properties are most useful.
● Ask the children to suggest ways of preventing the egg from breaking before splitting them into Research and Development (R&D) Teams.

Obtaining evidence
● Depending on time/resources, either allow children to choose their own materials to test, or allot materials to each group. Capsules and egg-onauts can then be wrapped in a range of test materials.
● As the children work, challenge them to be as innovative as possible. For example, what happens if the capsule is wrapped in clay or large elastic bands are wrapped around it to make a 'rubber' coat?
● Encourage at least one of the teams to carry out a test that simulates the protective materials on Apollo's capsule. Bubble wrap makes a good representation of the 'honeycombed' aluminium inner shell. Cork tiles can be cut up and taped to the bubble wrap to mimic the outer layer.
● If a material fails its initial test, then hand out a second egg and encourage children to

repeat the test, adding another layer of materials on top of the original.
● Children may also want to put their capsules inside additional containers. These can include hand-made boxes constructed using sheets of packing polystyrene, cardboard or cork tiles.
● Alternatively, they may like to use cardboard tubes which will hold the egg firmly, cocoa tins, which are strong but light or boxes which can be packed with 'loose fill' materials like packing peanuts.

Drawing together
● Round up with a short summary from a representative of each R&D team highlighting which materials were the most effective. *From our experiments, can we determine what common properties all of the successful materials have?*
● Finally, ask the children to draw their own space capsules, using what they've learned to inspire their designs. Encourage them to include labels for each part of the craft, describing the properties the materials must have.

Support
Before each test, help the children to use the photocopiable sheet to record the name of each material and its properties.

Extension
Inspire children to devise and test other ways of protecting the egg. For example, will the egg still break if it has less distance to fall or if it falls more slowly?
(Some space probes have parachutes to slow their descent.) Will the egg survive better if it's dropped in water or sand?

Scientific language
insulating – prevents heat entering or leaving an object

Fun with friction

Setting the context
Anuska has a new pet, Rover. However, Rover isn't a dog but the latest high-tech gadget designed to move around on the surface of alien worlds. Rover is the brain-child of Anuska's professor and, as a special assignment, she's been asked to test how well he moves over a range of different surfaces. "We don't know what the surface of the planet we hope to land on is like" explained Professor Moonbloom. "So we don't know whether to give Rover wheels, skis or a sledge base." Anuska smiled and thought, "This should be easy. After all, it's just having fun with friction."

The problem
Which method of 'locomotion' is most effective at reducing friction on a range of surfaces?

Objectives
To learn that friction is a type of force that slows moving objects.
To test ways of over-coming friction.

Background information
Any object moving in a straight line will continue to do so unless a **force** acts upon it. The unseen force that causes a rolling ball to stop, without any intervention, is called **friction**. 'Sliding friction' is created by two objects rolling over each other. We can reduce the amount of contact one object has with another by using wheels, skates, oil, water and ice as 'friction-busters'. Sometimes, however, we need friction. That's why shoes and tyres have treads. Tread increases the area in contact with the ground. This increases friction and stops us from falling over.

You will need
Thick cardboard; empty margarine tubs; pencils/lengths of dowel; double-sided sticky tape; glue; rulers; craft knives/scissors; long piece of smooth MDF or a table; a selection of rough and smooth textures to cover the MDF, such as sandpaper, tin foil; photocopiable pages 57 and 58.

Preparation
Ask children to bring in roller blades, sledges, scooters, radio-controlled cars or anything similar. Make space for the children to test their items on a smooth floor and on a length of carpet/textured paper as a contrasting surface.
Prepare a test 'track' ideally made from a long piece of smooth MDF, raised to at least 30°,

or a table, raised at one end. Cover with one of the rough or smooth textures to be tested first. Alternatively, mark out a track on the floor. As the floor is flat, children will need to push each vehicle with the same force every time to ensure experiments are fair.

Note: the introduction to this activity won't suit all groups. Rolling balls across a table covered in a range of textured papers, makes a good alternative.

Discussion and research
● Begin with a practical demonstration of friction.
● Allow the group to take turns to test their scooters and other items on a smooth surface. Then test a contrasting surface. Ensure the areas used are clutter-free and co-ordinate the activity carefully to avoid accidents and over-boisterous behaviour.
● After testing both surfaces, explain how friction works.
● Inspire children to discuss which surfaces/types of vehicle seemed to produce the most/least friction. Anuska's Rover needs to perform well over a range of surfaces. As we've just seen, this could be tricky!
● Speculate on whether wheels, skates or a sledge might work best on both rough and smooth surfaces, before taking a vote.

Obtaining evidence
● Demonstrate how to make the test vehicles:
● The Wheeled Rover:
1. Cut out four thick, cardboard wheels, 5cm in diameter. Cut out four square 'washers', 2cm x 2cm.
2. Find the centre of each wheel and make a hole using a sharp pencil.
3. Position the wheels on the tub. Mark where the holes lie. Make a smaller hole in each corner of the tub.
4. Carefully push the pencils through then tub.
5. Position the wheels. Ensure the holes are large enough to allow the wheels to spin easily. Add washers to hold the wheels in place.

6. Add a 'passenger' to weigh down the vehicle and test.
● The Ski Rover:
1. Remove the wheels.
2. Fashion a pair of skis from two strips of thick card, 2cm wide and $1\frac{1}{4}$ times the diameter of the tub. Round one end of each ski to make a blade.
3. Add a 'passenger' and test.
● The Sled Rover:
1. Remove the skis. Affix double-sided tape to the bottom of the tub.
2. Cut out a cardboard sled base, at least $1\frac{1}{4}$ times the size of the base of the tub. Curl up the front edge of the card then stick to the tub.
3. Add a 'passenger' and test.
● Set out the test area and experiment with each vehicle/surface in turn, noting carefully how far each Rover travels.

Drawing together
● Together discuss how well each of the test vehicles did. *Did any one vehicle perform well on all surfaces?*
● Finally, collate the results into a class data set.

Support
Make a display showing photographs/ drawings of vehicles with 'friction-busting' properties.

Extension
Slide a selection of (empty!) shoes/ trainers along a slippery test track. Consider how and why the amount of tread affects the amount of slide.

Scientific language
force - a type of energy which produces a change in the motion of an object.
friction - a force created by two objects rolling over each other.

Create a crater

Setting the context

Since finishing her report on Rover, Anuska has been hard at work. She's been worried that the Space Agency might send Rover to a planet for which it's not properly equipped. What if they give it wheels and the planet's surface was water - or worse, molten lava? Fortunately, Anuska has an idea. By studying photographs of the craters on the planet's surface, she thinks she'll be able to work out exactly what type of surface the Rover will find....

The problem

Can craters really help Anuska discover what a planet's surface is like?

Photo © Craig Jewell

Objectives

To describe, group and compare rocks and soils based on their behaviour and characteristics.
To compare everyday materials on the basis of their properties.

Background information

Even with powerful telescopes it can be hard to get a clear image of the details of a planet's surface. Often simple geology can tell us just as much as satellite images and radar. For example, rocks hitting soft, hard or clay-like surfaces all produce different craters. A planet with few or no craters is either very young or has a liquid/molten surface. Craters are caused when debris from space collides with the surface of a planet. There are many types of 'space debris' - comets made of ice, rocks called asteroids, and meteoroids which burn up in the atmosphere to create 'shooting stars'. Rocks that impact on a planet's surface are known as meteorites.

You will need

Plastic ice-cream tubs, numbered and filled 7cm deep with a selection of test materials such as fine builder's sand, fine/coarse gravel or shale, clay, peat, large aquarium-style rocks; newspaper or plastic sheets to protect surfaces; digital camera (optional); photocopiable page 59.
Per group: protective goggles; golf ball; tape measure; short plastic ruler.

Preparation

Create a display of crater images (optional). The Solar Views website provides an excellent selection of images of Earth craters, including information about the types of sands/soils in each region (www.solarviews.com/eng/ tercrate.htm#views). Google Images is also a good source of dramatic images, both terrestrial and extraterrestrial.

Photo © Krzysztof Snazyk

Discussion and research

● Begin by asking the children to look at and feel each of the substances in the tubs. Ask them to think about the texture of each substance - whether the granules are fine or coarse, heavy or light, dense or loosely packed.

● Work with them to sort the tubs into groups of materials that share similar textures. Help them to give reasons for their choices.

● Can they name each substance? Draw on the children's everyday experiences to decide if a substance is soil, sand, gravel or rock.

● Next, show the children the photocopiable sheet.

● Discuss the key features of the crater in the photograph and draw up a list of its 'characteristics'. The image shows the type of crater made by a golf ball dropped from a height of 122cm into a 7cm deep tub of fine builder's sand. (Children will need to use the same technique to get comparable results.)

● *Which of the substances we've just seen do you think would react like this if it was hit by a meteorite?*

Obtaining evidence

● To ensure a fair experiment (and to make sure that the children's tests resemble the crater on the photocopiable sheet) the golf ball meteorites will need to be dropped from 122cm.
This height should be measured, using a tape measure, for each test.

● Depending on time and resources, either ask each group to test every material, or allot one or two materials per group.

● If groups are sharing tubs, they will need to fill in any previous craters and smooth down the surface using the edge of a small ruler, before they begin their own test.

● Help the children to measure the width and depth of each crater, as well as making sketches to show the crater's overall shape.

● If a digital camera is available, you may like to take photographs of the craters. Images can then be used to make an annotated display that compares and contrasts the results of each test.

Drawing together

● *From our experiments, can we say which substance produced a crater similar to the one in the photograph?*

● Before the children give their answers, ask them to consider carefully all the evidence, including any measurements, sketches and photographs.

● If possible, compare the data from more than one test on the same substance. Consider how they are different/the same.

● Were the children correct? *Can craters really help Anuska discover what a planet's surface is like?*

● Finally, stimulate the children to write up their findings in the style of an encyclopaedia entry on 'Creating Craters'.

Support
Additional fun substances to test include: water, mud, thick porridge (dyed red to represent lava), ice, Silly Putty and cotton wool.

Extension
Experiment to discover whether the size, speed and angle of the golf ball affects the size and shape of a crater.

Don't drink the water!

Setting the context

Professor Moonbloom had spent the last year writing his epic *'DIY Book of Space Travel'*. The Professor knows that, in the past, when people settled in new, far away places they often had to make everything they needed to survive from scratch. "I believe that life in space for the first settlers will be just the same," he said, "which is why my book will be so useful". Anuska isn't so sure, but she has promised to help him write the next chapter, which is on food and drink. The only problem is how on Earth (or Mars) is she supposed to make a water filter?

The problem

How can you make a water filter?

Objectives

To describe changes that occur when materials are mixed.
To separate solid particles of different sizes using a sieve.
To separate solids from liquids by filtering.
To know that some solids dissolve in liquids to make solutions, while some do not.

Background information

A solution is made when we dissolve one or more substances (solutes) in a liquid called a solvent. Some solids don't dissolve completely - solid particles remain visible. This is an example of a **suspension**. The liquid produced when we filter a suspension is called a filtrate. Early attempts at purifying water focussed on removing these visible solids. Ancient Greeks filtered their water througha cloth bag. People of the Indus Valley used filters made from charcoal. The earliest large-scale water treatment plants in Britain used beds of sand. Today, the process is more complex - we add chemicals to kill germs, but it still begins with filtering and sieving.

You will need

Water; sieve; photocopiable page 60

Per group: 500ml or 1-litre plastic bottle with the end cut off and the sharp edges covered in tape; two empty mixing jugs; plastic spoons; selection of materials to make a 'dirty' solution/suspension and to filter the resulting liquids; jug of tap water labelled 'control'.

Safety Even if the water looks clean after the experiment, children should never drink it. (Explain that filtration only removes visible dirt. In reality, water would also need to be boiled or treated with chlorine tablets to make sure that there were no harmful microscopic substances in it.)

Preparation

Source a selection of materials to mix with water to make the solutions/suspensions. Include soil, shale/gravel, flour, rice and sand. For the filters, provide the children with a range of materials such as blotting paper, cotton wool, sand, shale/gravel, stones and clay. You may wish to ask the children to suggest and bring in their own suitable filter materials.

Discussion and research

● Show the children the flour and gravel and encourage them to describe how the two materials are the same/different. Mix the two solids together.
● *How easy will it be to separate these two solids? Can you suggest any ways of doing this?*
● Put the mixture in a sieve and demonstrate how the gravel and flour can be (relatively) quickly separated.
● Now imagine that we had added flour or gravel to water. *Would it be just as easy to separate?*
● This is the sort of problem that the Space Settlers of the future may have to cope with.
● Challenge the children to imagine that they have landed on a strange planet and have to make a filter which will be able to make the local water clean enough to drink.

Obtaining evidence

● Begin by making up a test solution using one of the finely-textured materials - such as soil, sand or flour.
● You'll need to agree how to make up the solution (e.g. how much sand per litre of water) to ensure that the experiments are fair.
● Encourage the children to note down what they observe.
● Then, split them into groups of Space Settlers.
● Demonstrate how to make a basic water filter:
1. Fill the neck-end of the plastic bottle with shale/gravel (ensure the shale/gravel particles are large enough to block bottle neck-end!)

2. Pour the dirty water into the plastic bottle.
3. Hold the neck-end over a second measuring jug, to collect the water.
4. Compare the filtrate with ordinary tap water (our **control**) and give it a score out of 5.
● *Can you make a more effective water filter?*
● Stimulate them to start by testing one filter at a time, noting how well each material performs.
● *Can you make your solution cleaner by combining materials?*

Drawing together

● Round up by encouraging the Settlers to take it in turns to share their findings with the rest of the group.
● Ask each group to repeat the experiment which produced the cleanest water. Then compare the group's samples.
● Together vote to decide which Settlers made the best water filter.
● Finally, inspire the children to write up their experiment in the form of an entry in *The DIY Book of Space Travel.*

Support
Work with the children to complete the photocopiable sheet showing what their finished water filter looked like.

Extension
Follow on by challenging the children to test their newly-made filters on a range of solutions and suspensions.

Scientific language
suspension – a liquid in which solid particles have been mixed but have not dissolved
control - a substance which is usually left unaltered for comparison with other test materials

Planet spotting

Setting the context

Anuska has always been fascinated by the planets, asteroids, comets and meteors that clutter up outer space. Unfortunately, what she really hates is homework (even if it is learning about her favourite subjects). This week, Professor Moonbloom has set her a particularly tricky task.

He wants Anuska to find a safe way of observing the Sun. That means that she can't look at it directly or even through sunglasses. What she needs is a little help from a friend or two....

The problem

How can the Sun be observed safely?

Objectives

To know that the Earth, Sun and Moon are approximately spherical.
To know that day and night are related to the spin of the Earth.
To understand how months and years are related to the orbits of the Earth and Moon.
To understand that light travels in a straight line from a light source.
To learn that some materials block light, causing shadows, and that some materials reflect light.

Photo © Rodolfo, Italy

Background information

Pinhole viewers behave like cameras. The hole acts as a lens and the paper as a viewer. Although not apparent with spherical objects, images produced will be upside down and back to front. The objects the children will be 'spotting' are not really planets. The Sun is a star - a huge ball of burning gases - positioned at the centre of our Solar System, 149,600,000 km away from Earth. The Moon is the Earth's only natural **satellite**, and sits 384,467 km from Earth. There are eight true planets. All orbit the Sun and are approximately spherical in shape. Moons **orbit** planets, rather than the Sun.

You will need

Per group: A4 sheet of cardboard; sticky tape; ruler; craft knife/scissors; aluminium foil; A4 sheet of white paper/card; thumb tack; tape measure; photographs of the

Earth, Moon and Sun.

Safety Children should be taught never to look directly at the Sun or even the Moon. To do so can cause permanent and irreversible eye damage.

Preparation
If the Sun is not visible, find a picture of the Sun on the internet to show on the whiteboard or on an OHP.

Discussion and research
● Begin with a quick game of 'Solar System Challenge'. Hold up the pictures of the Earth, Moon and Sun and ask the children to come up with five statements about each. For example: the Earth, Sun and Moon are (almost) round in shape; the Sun is very bright; the Earth travels around the Sun; the Moon travels around the Earth, the Sun can be dangerous, and so on. Draw out information by allowing children to make suggestions, adding correct statements to the whiteboard.
● Then, remind them about Anuska's problem. *What safe ways of observing the Sun can you think of?* Encourage the children to make suggestions.

Obtaining evidence
● We can't look at the Sun (or the Moon) directly, it's too dangerous, but we can look at the shadow it casts by making a pinhole viewer.
● Simple pinhole viewers can be constructed out of an A4 sheet of cardboard, with a pin hole placed in the centre. This is our lens. Use an A4 sheet of white paper/ card as a viewer.
● On a sunny day, take the children outside and divide them into pairs.
● Children should stand with their backs to the Sun; one child holding the lens and the other holding the viewer. The image of the Sun can be focused on the viewer by moving it back and forth until an image appears.
● Results using this simple viewer may be blurry at best, but this basic model is a good starting point and offers groups the chance

to discuss, refine and compare various designs.
● For a sharper image, cut a square in the centre of some cardboard and tape a sheet of aluminium foil (or any very thin but opaque material) over the hole. Make the pin hole in the foil and repeat the experiment.
● On overcast days the activity can be carried out indoors using an over-head projector or whiteboard. Display an image of the Sun on the whiteboard/wall. (Ensure the room is dark and clutter free to avoid accidents!)

Drawing together
● After the activity, discuss how effective each pinhole design was.
● *Why do we need pinhole viewers to look at the Sun? How did we make our viewers? What did we see? Why?*
● Round up by challenging children to use books and the Internet to find out about the Sun/Moon and present their findings in a class display.

Support
Make 'Sun Safety' posters emphasising why we should never look directly at the Sun.

Extension
Challenge the children to discover how large the Sun really is. Measure the diameter of the image on the viewer and the distance from the lens to the viewer. Divide the two and multiply by the distance of the Sun/Moon from the Earth.

Scientific language
satellite - an object which revolves around a planet.
orbit - the path taken by any planet or satellite around another.

Splash down!

- Complete this record sheet carefully.

[Attach your sample here]

Sample: _____

Properties: • _____

• _____

• _____

Did the egg break? Yes/No. _____

[Attach your sample here]

Sample: _____

Properties: • _____

• _____

• _____

Did the egg break? Yes/No. _____

[Attach your sample here]

Sample: _____

Properties: • _____

• _____

• _____

Did the egg break? Yes/No. _____

Teacher's notes: This page can be used as an individual worksheet, or enlarged and used with whole groups.

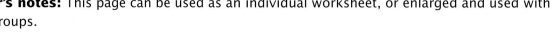

Fun with friction 1

a)

_____
_____
_____

Test 1 _____
_____

b)

_____
_____
_____

Test 1 _____
_____

c)

_____
_____
_____

Test 1 _____
_____

d)

_____
_____
_____

Test 1 _____
_____

e)

_____
_____
_____

Test 1 _____
_____

f)

_____
_____
_____

Test 1 _____
_____

Teacher's notes: This page can be used as an aide-memoir to help children as they make their test vehicles. Space has been left for children to note down what's happening in each picture, plus the results of their tests.

Fun with friction 2

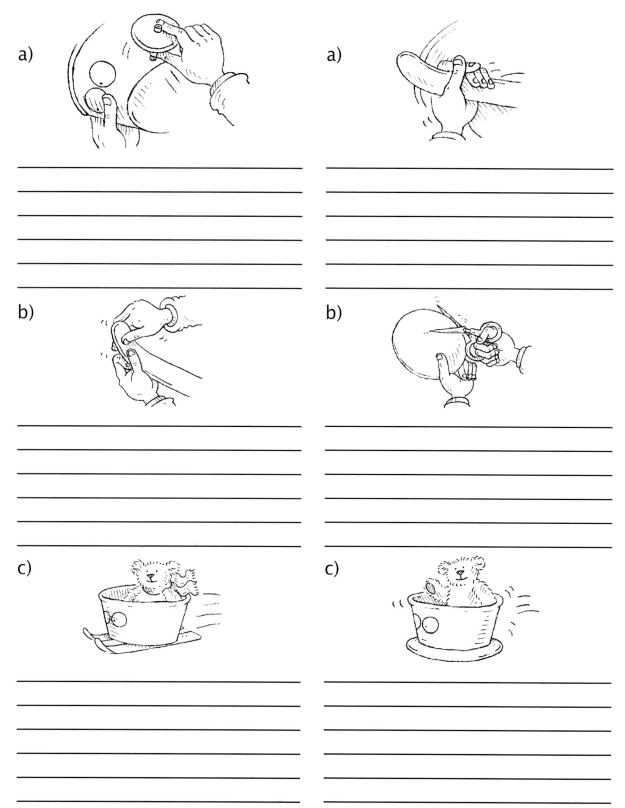

a)

_____
_____
_____
_____
_____

a)

_____
_____
_____
_____
_____

b)

_____
_____
_____
_____
_____
_____

b)

_____
_____
_____
_____
_____
_____

c)

_____
_____
_____
_____
_____
_____

c)

_____
_____
_____
_____
_____
_____

Teacher's notes: This page can be used as an aide-memoir to help children as they make their test vehicles. Space has been left for children to note down what's happening in each picture, plus the results of their tests.

Create a crater

Don't drink the water!

- Complete this picture of your finished water filter. Then write about what you did.

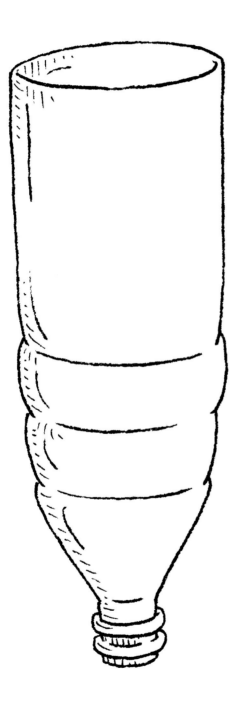

_____

_____

_____

_____

_____

_____

_____

_____

_____

_____

_____

_____

_____

_____

_____

_____

_____

_____

Teacher's notes: This page can be used as an individual worksheet, or enlarged and used with whole groups.

Chapter Four

That's magic!

The experiments in this chapter use the character of Mohit the Magical to introduce children to some of the weird, wonderfuland seemingly 'magical' things that can be done with everyday materials and a little appliance of science.

● We begin with a theme introduced in Chapter 3: 'Materials and their properties' by taking a look at 'mixing and changing materials'. In **Smile please!** the children investigate the non-reversible, chemical changes that happen when light sensitive paper is exposed to the Sun. In **Rain, rain, go away!** we explore reversible changes, examining with children evaporation and condensation as part of the water cycle, by making their own indoor rainmakers. **A tight squeeze** looks at the differences between the three states of matter: specifically how solids, liquids and gases flow and the volume that they fill.

● **A tight squeeze** can also be used in conjunction with **Magical magnets** to create a body of work that deals with 'Types of force'. Children who have already carried out the experiments on pages 44-45 (**Roaring rockets**) and 48-49 (**Fun with friction**) will be familiar with different types of force and these additional pages give the opportunity to round up work on the topic. **A tight squeeze**, which involves getting eggs into bottles, looks at how differences in pressure can create suction. While **Magical magnets** gives the children the chance to make their own UFOs (Unidentified Floating Objects), using the forces generated by magnetic fields to create magnetic levitation.

● The final two activities, **Abracadabra!** and **Turning lead into gold**, act as a fun introduction to the topic of 'Electricity'. The first deals with the sometimes shocking properties of static electricity. The second introduces children to simple circuits while investigating electro-plating. **Turning lead into gold** can also be used to explore the topic of changing materials further.

● We round up with five photocopiable pages which are intended to support and enhance learning. These include a water conservation game based on Snakes and Ladders and simple sentence strips to aid comprehension.

Page **61**

Smile please!

Setting the context

Mohit the Magical is a whizz at achieving the seemingly unachievable, but even his biggest fan, Abee, doesn't believe that he can really take photographs without a camera. "Ah!" laughed Mohit, "It's true - ordinary people do need cameras to take photographs, but I'm a magician, so all I need is to wave my magic wand over this piece of paper, and hey presto!" Now Abee knows that there's no such thing as magical paper. Can you help him figure out how Mohit's 'magic' really works?

The problem

How can we make 'photographs' without a camera?

Objectives

To know that some changes are non-reversible and may result in the formation of a new substance or material.
To learn that some materials block light, causing shadows, and that some materials reflect light.

Background information

Sun print papers are similar to 'cyanotypes' which were once used to make blueprints (cyan is a type of blue). The paper is covered in a thin layer of iron **salts**. When exposed to light, these salts undergo a permanent chemical change and turn back into a metal. (They're 'reduced' to their metallic state.) **Opaque** objects will block light, leaving sharp outlines on the paper. Semi-transparent and **translucent** objects let some light through, producing more interesting and dramatic prints. Washing the Sun paper in water 'fixes' it by removing any unused salts. This stops further chemical reactions.

You will need

A sunny day; supply of clean water; Sun print paper*; blue construction paper, of roughly the same size and shade as the Sun print paper; assorted items with which to make Sun prints; a 'magic wand'; stop-watch; two 'fixing trays' containing cold water (paint trays are ideal); photocopiable page 74.

* Sun print paper kits can be bought from craft stores and educational suppliers.

Preparation

Collect some interesting objects to be used to make Sun prints e.g. leaves, shells, springs, paper clips (Include opaque, translucent and transparent items.)
Prepare two packages: one containing a sheet of Sun print paper, the other containing a sheet of construction paper.

Discussion and research

● This is an ideal outdoor activity, so if you have
a suitable space and a sunny day, begin by taking the children outside.
● Ask for three volunteers:
Hand the package containing Sun print paper to the first volunteer.
Hand the package containing construction paper to the second volunteer. These are 'magical papers' and the packages need to be kept tightly closed to stop the magic seeping out!
Help the third volunteer to select two items from the display with similar 'properties' and hand one to each of their class mates.
● Hand out the water-filled, fixing trays and place them on the ground.
● Ask the child with the Sun paper to wave the wand over their package and say the

magic words "*cyanotype*". This will magically 'charge' the paper. We'll leave the other paper 'uncharged'.

● Start the stopwatch. This is the cue for children to take out their papers and place them on the ground with the chosen object on top. This needs to be done as quickly as possible.

● When you stop the watch, children should put their papers in the fixing trays for between one and three minutes. This washes off the remaining 'magic'.

Obtaining evidence

● Together discuss what happened. *Was it really magic? What else could have caused the reaction? Why didn't both papers change?*

● Mohit likes to use science to baffle his friends, but we all know that the papers weren't really magical. However, one of them was 'chemical'!

● Briefly explain how Sun prints work, then allow the children to experiment further for themselves.

● Encourage them to make notes of how they made their prints including what objects they used, how long they exposed the paper for and whether they placed it in direct light or shade.

● Challenge the children to compare what happens when they vary the exposure time and the location/time of day.

● They may also like to compare the type of prints made using objects that completely block light with those that are partially transparent.

Drawing together

● Round up by asking the children to mount their best Sun print, together with a brief note explaining how it was made.

● Display the children's work in a class gallery, having mounted their prints on the photocopiable sheet. Encourage them to discuss the merits of each print.

● Consider why some prints worked better than others. *Can we draw any conclusions about the quality of prints produced by different objects (transparent, opaque and translucent) and why? Are there any ideal 'conditions' in which to make Sun prints?*

Support

Make foot and hand Sun prints. Take photographs of each stage of the process. The foot and hand prints can be glued to the frame on the photocopiable sheet and displayed together with the photographs to show how the prints were created. Encourage the children to think of a label for each step of the process.

Extension

Compare the effects of other natural and artificial light sources on the paper.

Scientific language

salts - formed by a chemical reaction between an acid and a base

opaque – materials that do not allow light to pass through

translucent - materials that allow light to pass through, but 'jumble' it up so resulting images are often distorted

Rain, rain, go away!

Setting the context

The best thing about being a magician (or a very clever scientist) is that Mohit always gets invited to the coolest parties. While other magicians pull rabbits out of hats or make their beautiful assistants vanish, Mohit usually devises something much more interesting to entertain his fans... and today, he has big plans. He's working on a new trick that involves making it rain - indoors! His mum thinks he's crazy, but Mohit knows that all he needs is a little knowledge and just the right 'spell ingredients' ....

The problem
Can we make it rain indoors?

Objectives
To know about reversible changes, including dissolving, melting, boiling and freezing.
To recognise the differences between how solids, liquids and gases flow and the volume that they fill.
To learn about the part played by evaporation and condensation in the water cycle.
To describe changes that happen when objects are heated or cooled.
To learn that temperature is a measure of how hot or cold objects are.

Background information
Water is the only substance that exists naturally as a solid, liquid and **vapour**. Its state depends on the speed its **molecules** move. Cold molecules slow down and 'bunch up'. Warm molecules speed up and 'spread out'. That's why boiling water **evaporates** and turns into vapour. It **condenses** back into liquid as it cools. Evaporation and condensation happen continually as part of the water cycle. During this cycle, water heated by the Sun evaporates, rises, hits cold air, cools, condenses into clouds and falls back to Earth as precipitation (rain). In this way, the Earth's limited supply of water is constantly recycled.

You will need
Water; kettle; oven mitt; deep, metal baking tray; made-to-measure 'viewer'; four 500ml plastic bottles, $\frac{3}{4}$ filled with water and then frozen; photocopiable pages 75 and 76.

Safety Boiling water and steam can burn. Supervise children closely.

Preparation
● The viewer is a strong, rectangular box, with no top and a panel cut from one long side. Four, wide, v-shaped notches, cut into the long sides of the top of the box, hold the frozen water bottles in place. Water-proof by painting with PVA glue and, if necessary, reinforce with additional card. Alternatively, use foam card which won't buckle when wet.
● Dimensions depend on the size of the bottles/baking tray, however, basic construction is as follows:
1. Source a strip of very thick card, 24cm high and at least four times the width of the tray. Divide this into four sections - short, long,

short, long - with 2cm tabs at either end.
2. The width of each short section should be 2cm shorter than the height of a plastic bottle. The width of each long section should be the same width as the baking tray.

3. Cut four, wide, v-shaped notches along the top of each long section.
4. Cut a panel out of one of the long sides.
5. Score the card, fold and make a box. Check the tray fits inside and that the notches line up. If not, adjust.
6. Staple along the tabs and reinforce joins with sticky tape.

7. Paint a sky scene inside and stick cotton wool 'clouds' on the frozen bottles (optional).

Discussion and research
● Show the children water as a liquid and a solid. Together consider: *What do these two things have in common? How can we turn water into ice - and back again? What other state can we find water in?*
● Boil the kettle until steam is visible. Help children describe what they see and work out the science behind it.
● Explain briefly about the water cycle and the part played by evaporation and condensation.
● We can see steam coming from the kettle because hot vapour condenses rapidly when it hits cooler air. This doesn't happen as

quickly in the water cycle, but the process is the same.
● Challenge the children to use their new knowledge to work out a 'scientific' definition of rain, such as 'rain is condensed water vapour'.

Obtaining evidence
● Remind the children what they saw when the kettle boiled. *Is it possible to make rain (condensed water vapour) indoors?* Take a vote before setting up the viewer.
● Fill the tray with boiling water. Put the frozen bottles in place. (Stand well back, in case the bottles fall and splash boiling water.) It should only take a few minutes to 'make rain'.

Drawing together
● Round up by asking: *How successful was our 'Rainmaker'? How could we get better results?*
Have we made 'rain'? (Think about our definition.)
● Finish by discussing water conservation and playing conservation snakes and ladders on photocopiable page 75.

Support
Use photocopiable page 76 to reinforce the children's understanding of the water cycle.

Extension
Inspire the children to design posters showing 'The water cycle at work'.

Scientific language
vapour - the gaseous state of a substance which is solid or liquid at normal temperatures
molecule - the simplest chemical unit
evaporate - change from a liquid or solid to a vapour
condense - change from a vapour to a liquid or solid

A tight squeeze

Setting the context

Mohit the Magical may spend a lot of his time poring over books and testing experiments, but he still likes to have a good laugh. In fact he's always playing tricks on his family, and this morning is probably his best ever! When Mum sat down to breakfast she found that her hard-boiled egg was inside the ketchup bottle.

She's been trying to figure just how the trick was done, but she has to admit, she's stumped. However Mohit has left her one clue: pull, don't push. What can he mean?

The problem

How can you get an egg into a ketchup bottle without breaking the egg or the bottle?

Objectives

To recognise the differences between how solids, liquids and gases flow and the volume that they fill.
To describe changes that happen when objects are heated or cooled.
To learn that temperature is a measure of how hot or cold objects are.

Background information

Air molecules move constantly. How much they move determines how much volume the air takes up. In common with most substances, air contracts when cooled. This is because cooling causes molecules to slow down and 'bunch up'. Warming the air speeds up the molecules. Faster molecules need more space to move around in, so hot air

expands. As we heat the air inside the bottle, it too expands. There is limited space in the bottle so 'excess' air is pushed out. When we remove the heat, the air begins to cool and **contract**. This leaves an 'empty space' in the bottle, which creates an area of low **pressure** that pulls the egg inside.

You will need

Hot water; hard-boiled, shelled eggs; washing-up liquid; 535g glass ketchup bottles, with a neck at least 3.5cm in diameter; stopwatches; digital camera and PC (optional).

Safety Take the opportunity to reinforce safety messages when using very hot water.

Preparation

Hard boil the eggs.

Discussion and research

● Begin by handing round the pre-prepared egg in a bottle.
● Show the children an ordinary hard-boiled

egg so they see and test for themselves that it will not fit through the bottle neck.

● *Can you suggest any ways of getting the egg into the bottle?* Some children may suggest heating the bottle, which is a good idea, and offers the opportunity to discuss how most substances will expand when heated. Others may suggest greasing the egg to reduce friction.

● Depending on the size of the bottle/egg some of these suggestions may work! However, remind them of the clue Mohit gave: pull, don't push. *If we can't push the egg into the bottle, how can we possibly pull it?*

● Make a list of further ideas before showing the children how it's done.

Obtaining evidence

● The trickiest part of this experiment is finding a bottle with a neck just the right size. A medium-sized, shelled egg and a tall, 535g glass ketchup bottle with a neck at least 3.5cm in diameter works best. Salad dressing and olive oil bottles are good alternatives.

● As the water needs to be very hot for this experiment, you may prefer to run it as a demonstration rather than a group activity. However, if children are allowed to try for themselves, it's recommended that bottles are both filled and emptied by an adult.

● Fill the bottle with very hot tap water and leave to stand until the glass becomes hot to the touch.

● Pre-lubricate the egg with washing up liquid to reduce friction. (If the children have already done work on friction, then you may like to discuss this with them first.)

● Pour out the hot water and place the egg, pointed end down, onto the bottle neck as quickly as possible. **Suction** should start work

immediately, although it can take up to half an hour for the egg to be pulled completely inside the bottle.

● Add an element of competition by encouraging children to time how long it takes for their egg to be sucked into the bottle.

● Further ideas:
Experiment with bottles of different volumes (but the same diameter neck) to discover which works best. *Do larger bottles generate more suction?*
Consider why.
Repeat the experiment with an un-shelled egg. This is possible by softening the shell in vinegar overnight (see pages 14-15).

Drawing together

● After the experiment, review the ideas that the children originally came up with. Were any correct?

● Finally, go on to explain how gases expand and contract, creating differences in pressure.

Support
Viewing the experiment using time-lapse photography can be both fun and informative. Take digital photographs of the egg and bottle every ten seconds. Download images to a PC and re-play at speed to make a movie.

Extension
Challenge children to write an explanation, in less than 100 words, of what Mohit's clue meant: how was the egg 'pulled' into the bottle?

Scientific language
expand - to become bigger
contract - to become smaller
pressure - the force applied by one object on another
suction - 'pull' created by a region of low pressure

Magical magnets

Setting the context

Mohit loves magnets. In fact they're h
favourite 'magical' item. He always us
them in his act because the effects
achieved by using a magnet's natural
forces of attraction and repulsion alwa,
amaze his audience. However, today it's
Mohit's turn to be surprised. A friend in
Shanghai has just e-mailed him some

photographs of a 'levitating' train. As a
magician, Mohit has tried making chairs
and dogs float, but he knows that's just a
trick. Yet, this train really does float and,
apparently, the secret is magnetism.

The problem
How can magnets make things 'levitate'?

Objectives

To learn about the forces of magnetic
attraction and repulsion.
To identify and measure types of force.

Background information

Magnetism is a type of force believed to be
created by the movement of electrons inside
atoms. If we lay a bar magnet on a piece of
paper and sprinkle iron filings on top, 'lines
of force' are revealed travelling from the
magnet's North pole to its South. Alike poles
repel; unalike attract, giving magnets many
interesting properties. 'Mag-lev' (magnetic
levitation) occurs when the forces of
repulsion and **attraction** are balanced. This
is very difficult because the force of
attraction is slightly stronger than that of
repulsion, which is why magnets tend to flip
over. Mag-lev trains use an electric current to
create a stable magnetic field. As the current
increases, so does the field, until there's
enough force to lift the train.

You will need

Selection of magnets* of varying sizes and
shapes, including bar magnets and magnetic

marbles; paper-clips; compasses and other
materials which will be attracted to magnets
or can be magnetised.

Per group: sheets of thick cardboard; double-
sided sticky tape; at least eight ferrite
magnets; scissors/craft knife; pencil;
photocopiable page 77.

*Permanent, medium strength, bi-polar,
ferrite magnets work best, such as round
20mm diameter magnets with a counter-sunk
central hole. (This makes it easier for young
children to identify alike poles.) Supplies can
be bought from companies such as
www.uk-magnet.com

Safety Never use Neodymium magnets with
young children. They are much more
powerful, but have such an incredible
attractive force that fingers can be seriously
damaged if caught between them.

Preparation

For each group, make a transparent tube
using the central section of a 500ml plastic
bottle. Seal any sharp edges with tape.

Discussion and research

● Ask for volunteers to take on the roles of Magician(s) and Assistant(s). Together, spend a little time working out a short 'magic act' using some of the magnets. For example, magnetic marbles look like ordinary magnets yet attract and repel each other and other objects. Paper clips can be made to 'dance' by putting them on a sheet of card and moving magnets beneath. Ordinary metallic objects can be temporarily magnetised by stroking them (in one direction only) with a magnet.

● After the demonstration, challenge the children to explain what they've just seen.

● Then, work together to draw up a list of all the properties that magnets have, which they have just seen demonstrated. Emphasise the fact that this isn't magic but magnetism, which relies on the forces of repulsion and attraction.

Obtaining evidence

● Remind the children of what they saw during the class magic show.

● Using what they know, invite them to speculate about how 'mag-lev' trains might work.

● Although we don't have access to an electro magnet, we can make a model to demonstrate magnetic levitation at work:

1. Hand out the pre-prepared transparent tubes, a selection of magnets, plus the

cardboard, scissors and double-sided sticky tape.
2. Draw around the bottom of the tube to make four card circles.
3. Cut them out carefully, and trim them down until they fit snugly inside the tube. Glue together. (Children may like to paint the card silver and glue on a bottle lid to give a more UFO shape.)
4. Cut out a square of card and draw a circle in the middle.
5. Using double-sided tape, stick four magnets in the centre of the circle. Ensure that

they all have the same pole facing upwards. Tape the card to the tube.
6. Stick four more magnets onto the cardboard circle.

Ensure that they all have the same facing pole upwards but opposite to those on the base.

● Test out the UFOs (Unidentified Floating Objects).

● As they work, encourage children to experiment with different numbers of magnets and different poles to see which produces the best 'mag-lev' force.

Drawing together

● Hand out copies of the photocopiable sheet. Use it to create a 'web page' explaining how and why magnets make things levitate.

Support

Ask the children to make posters advertising Mohit's latest magic show, featuring his 'Magnetic Marvels'. Encourage them to include all the seemingly magical properties of magnets.

Extension

Ask the children to create additional web pages on any of the topics listed in the hyperlink boxes (see page 77).

Scientific language

repulsion - a force of push
attraction - a force of pull

Abracadabra!

Setting the context

Mohit's trick to make indoor rain was a huge hit, so he's decided to start work on a new idea - and it's a big one! "If everyone loved the rain trick," he mused to himself, "then imagine what they'll think of indoor lightning!" The problem is, lightning is treacherous stuff and he doesn't really want to put anyone in danger. Then, suddenly, one morning, as he was combing his hair, he had a 'flash' of inspiration. Now he just needs to test out some materials...

The problem
Which materials produce the best 'lightning'?

Objectives
To learn about static electricity.
To understand that some items are better conductors or insulators than others.

Background information
Everything is made of **atoms**. In the centre of every atom is a nucleus that contains positive protons and negative electrons. When we comb our hair, electrons are transferred from our hair to the comb. As with magnets, these opposite charges attract, so the negatively charged comb attracts positively charged hair (or any 'neutral' surface). Some charges repel, so our hair stands up on end as each hair is repelled by the next. When an object loses or gains enough electrons, it takes on an electric charge. This static electricity often jumps from one item to another, creating visible sparks. This happens on a much bigger scale to create lightning.

You will need
A selection of very large, flat 'conductive' pie tins, baking trays, or sheets of aluminium foil; large sheets of flat, insulating material such as expanded polystyrene, Plexiglas or any rigid plastic packing material (bigger than the metallic trays); plastic comb; pieces of fake fur; selection of items to test; stopwatches; round-edged, metal ruler; tissue paper (optional).

Safety Real lightning can kill. Remind children of safe behaviour during storms.

Preparation

Find some photographs or video footage of lightning (optional). Excellent images are available to view online via Google Images and Google Video.

Discussion and research

● Ask a child to comb their hair vigorously for a minute. Then ask the child to hold their comb over their hair. Everyone should see the hair being 'pulled' towards the comb. Alternatively, hold the comb over a piece of tissue paper to see it lift up.

● Together consider: *What's happening to the hair? Why is it attracted to the comb? What has this got to do with lightning?*

● Although Mohit would insist it's magic, the secret is actually static electricity.

● Explain that, although the static electricity produced during a lightning strike is immense, it's generated by the same forces of repulsion and attraction that affect our hair and the comb.

● Scientists are still struggling to understand the exact details, but it begins when water molecules in the clouds collide and lose electrons. The cloud becomes electrically charged, just like the comb. When the particles meet, the discharge of energy is so big, it can be seen as lightning.

Obtaining evidence

● Begin by demonstrating our Lightning Machine, before challenging the children to repeat the experiment for themselves.

● If it can be done safely, darken the room during the demonstration as this makes it easier to see any 'sparks'. The experiment will also work better in a dry atmosphere as damp air acts as a conductor and helps the electrons to 'dissipate'.

1. Place the sheet of polystyrene/plastic on a flat surface.
2. Rub it vigorously for at least one minute with the fake fur.
3. Hold the baking tray/pie tin 6cm above the polystyrene and drop it on top.

4. Using the round-edged metal ruler, touch the edge of the tray/pie tin. (Using a blunt metallic object or a finger will hurt!)
5. The children should hear a crackle and, if there's a big enough static charge, see a spark.

● Bigger sparks can be produced by repeating the experiment while holding the polystyrene in the air.

● Encourage children to test a range of different conductive and insulating materials, making sure they rub each one for the same amount of time, to see which produces the best lightning.

Drawing together

● Ask the children to take turns to demonstrate their most successful experiment. Together decide which materials produced the best results. (They may like to devise their own 'lightning scale' as a measure of how bright/large the sparks or crackles were.)

● *What happened when we rubbed the polystyrene? What happened to the tray/pie tin when it was dropped on top? Why did the polystyrene hold a good charge? Why was the tray/pie tin a good conductor? What has this got to do with how lightning is 'made'?*

Support
Explore other fun properties of static, such as how 'charged' balloons will stick to walls.

Extension
Challenge the children to write definitions of the following words: static electricity; attraction; repulsion; lightning.

Scientific language
atom - the smallest particle of matter

Turning lead into gold

Setting the context

Mohit the Magical has spent his life (all nine years of it) searching for answers to some of the BIG questions. Why was it harder to get out of bed on a school day, than at the weekend? Why did his sister spend an hour in the bathroom every morning? And why did mum *always* decide to vacuum up when Doctor Who was on TV? But the biggest question of all was one that had puzzled alchemists for centuries. How to turn lead into gold! Mohit figured he was already half way there; he just needed some help to test his ideas.

The problem

Is it really possible to change one metal into another?

Objectives

To know about reversible changes, including dissolving, melting, boiling and freezing.
To know that some solids dissolve in liquids to make solutions, while some do not.
To construct simple circuits to make electrical devices work.
To represent circuits using drawings and symbols.

Background information

Electroplating uses electricity to cause chemical change. To work, electricity must flow in a **circuit** from the positive terminal, through the **electrolyte** solution, to the negative **terminal**. The item to be coated (the cathode) is connected to the negative terminal and placed in the solution. Another piece of metal (the anode) is attached to the positive terminal. The anode is always made from the same metal as that dissolved in the solution. Opposites attract, so as electricity passes through the circuit, positively charged metal ions in the solution are attracted to the cathode. The result is a layer of metal 'plating'. For safety, we're using vinegar, which is mild acetic acid.

You will need

A number of 'plated' items.
Per child/group: measuring equipment; stirring rod; jam jar/glass beaker; two 30cm lengths of insulated wire with around 5cm of insulation stripped from each end; 4.5v battery with flat terminal connections; zinc metal strip; copper metal strip; crocodile clips; photocopiable page 78.

Preparation

Prepare the electrolyte solution by mixing 100g/per litre of Epsom Salts plus 120g/per litre of sugar in vinegar. Place a zinc 'elemental metal strip' in the solution and leave for at least two hours. Zinc fishing weights or well-cleaned copper (pre-1992) pennies work as an alternative.

Discussion and research

● Hand out a selection of plated items. Ask the children to think about how each object looks and feels. Although these items may look different, they have one thing in common. Beneath the shiny outer layer is a much cheaper metal.

● In *Harry Potter and the Philosopher's Stone* Nicolas Flamel has a stone that changes lead into gold (the side effect is the elixir of eternal life!). Mohit knows it's impossible to live forever, but he believes he may be able to change lead into gold.

● Encourage the children to discuss whether they think it's possible, giving reasons for their decisions.

● Explain that although we don't have any real lead or gold we can still test Mohit's ideas.

Obtaining evidence

● Demonstrate how to carry out the experiment:

1. Fill the jam jar to within 2cm of the top with the solution.
2. Take the lengths of wire and clean the exposed ends carefully.
3. Attach the copper strip to the end of one piece of wire. Attach the other end to the battery's negative terminal.
4. Attach one end of the second piece of wire to the zinc strip, and the other to the positive terminal.
5. Put both metals in the jar.

● After the demonstration, split Mohit's 'Apprentices' into groups and ask them to work together to select and lay out their equipment.

● Children should see results after 15 minutes. Success depends on the current, the length of time objects are left in the solution,

and the strength of the solution. A black deposit indicates too much current (3-6 volts is sufficient).

● When the copper strip is removed it should have 'changed' into zinc - or has it?

Drawing together

● Encourage the Apprentices to share their findings. Note down how many groups saw a change in the copper.

● Together, consider all the 'variables' that may have affected their success: How well the solution was made. How the equipment was chosen/set up. What was seen/heard during the experiment. Whether tests were repeated to ensure accuracy.

● *Have we proved our hypothesis?* (A chemical 'change 'has occurred but the copper strip is only 'plated'.)

● Round up by asking the Apprentices to use the photocopiable sheet to write up their experiment in the style of an ancient spell book, including a clearly annotated diagram of the electric circuit.

Support
Pre-prepare batches of the solution.

Extension
Help the children to vary the circuit and test what happens. For example, use batteries in sequence or swap the terminals around to repeat (and reverse?) the experiment.

Scientific language
circuit - the path an electric current takes
electrolyte - a solution which electricity can pass through
terminal - the point where electricity enters and leaves a circuit

Smile please!

■SCHOLASTIC
www.scholastic.co.uk

Rain, rain, go away ! 1

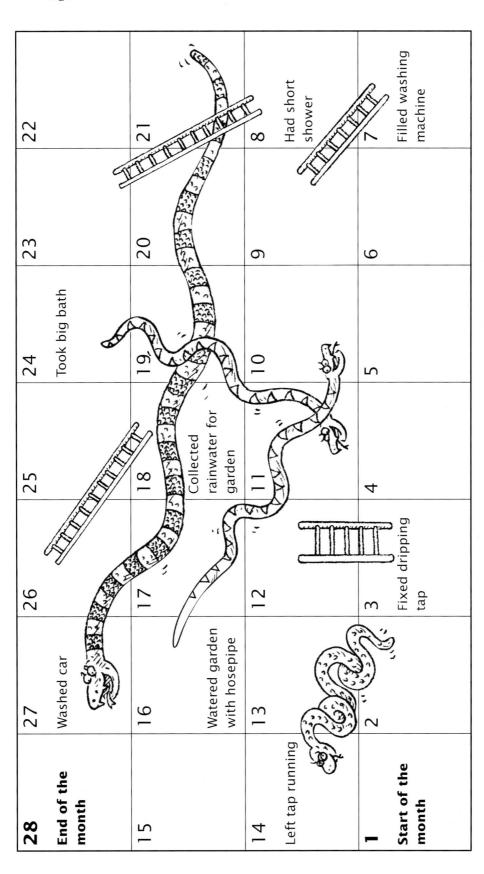

28 End of the month	27 Washed car	26	25	24 Took big bath	23	22
15	16	17	18	19	20	21
14	13	12	11	10 Collected rainwater for garden	9	8 Had short shower
1 Start of the month	2 Left tap running	3 Fixed dripping tap	4	5	6	7 Filled washing machine

Extra text visible in grid: Watered garden with hosepipe

Teacher's notes: Enlarge to A3 and play in teams or provide enough copies to allow individuals to play against each other.

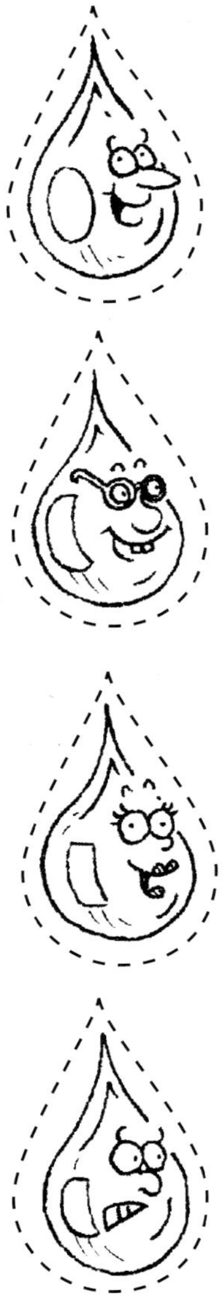

PHOTOCOPIABLE *Creative Activities for Scientific Enquiry: Ages 7-11*

Rain, rain, go away! 2

- Arrange these sentences in the correct order.

Water vapour rises into the air.

Water in rivers, lakes and oceans is warmed by the Sun.

Water in rivers, lakes and oceans is warmed by the Sun.

Water falls to Earth as rain.

As it rises, water vapour starts to cool.

Warm water starts to evaporate.

Rain water collects in rivers, lakes and oceans.

Water vapour condenses into clouds.

Teacher's notes: With very young children, this page can be enlarged to use with whole groups.

Magical magnets

- Mohit's Marvellous Rainmaker: You need never take a shower again!
- Elephant in a bottle! Astound your friends. Click here to find out more!

How compasses work

The North Pole

Uses of magnets

How to make a magnet

Ye curious spelle to turn lead into gold

SCHOLASTIC
www.scholastic.co.uk

Chapter Five

Eye spy

In this chapter we introduce children to the character of Jane Blond, Super Spy. Using situations from Jane's fictional life, children are lead through six, espionage-themed experiments. As with previous chapters, activities take a wide variety of approaches, from model making, to 'test and discover' experiments, from role play to discussions. They are all designed to demonstrate some of the more fun, yet practical applications of science.

● **All very hush hush** and **Up periscope!** deal with the themes of 'Light and sound'. The first encourages children to consider how sound waves travel through different mediums, before making and testing their own listening devices. The second explores how light can be reflected, refracted and absorbed. Children then go on to use reflected light to make a working spy 'scope.

● In **Must dot-dot, dash-dash** we return to the topic of electricity introduced in Chapter 4. Using just a few lengths of wire, a paperclip and two drawing pins, children are challenged to make their own battery-powered telegraph machines with which to send Morse code messages. **Must dot-dot, dash-dash** can also be used in conjunction with **Turning lead into gold** (pages 72-73) to demonstrate how quickly simple electrical circuits can be made.

● **Secret messages**, is a 'test and discover' experiment in which our fledgling spies are challenged to make the perfect 'invisible ink' with which to send clandestine reports.

● In **All in a day's work**, children are inspired to document 'A day in the life of our school', by recording the 'periodic changes' that happen over the course of an average day. In **Fantastic forensics,** children are presented with a crime scene to investigate. Both of these activities are give children the chance to draw on and consolidate the skills of research, observation, investigation and evaluation that they have developed over the course of their work from this book. **All in a day's work** can also be used with **Planet spotting** (pages 54-55), to create a body of work on the topic of 'The Earth and beyond'.

● The photocopiable resources include a mix of spy-themed worksheets, model templates and additional follow on activities.

All very hush hush

Setting the context

You've probably seen those films where the secret agent uses some great gadget to foil the plan of the evil villain. Unfortunately, as Super Spy Jane Blond knows, real life isn't always so simple. For example, her arch-nemesis, Dr Maybee has just sent her a mysterious package - and it's ticking! Before she opens it, she needs to have a better idea of what's inside, but she daren't use any of her latest gadgets in case they affect the contents. Perhaps she can find something useful in her kitchen.

The problem

How can you make a listening device using everyday kitchen items?

Objectives

To know that sound needs to travel through a medium such as air, metal or glass to reach our ears.
To understand that sounds are made when objects vibrate, although we may not always be able to see this.
To learn how the volume of a sound can be changed.

Background information

When objects make sounds, they vibrate. This, in turn, makes the substance surrounding the object, called the medium, vibrate. It's these vibrations that the sensitive organs inside our ears detect. If there's no medium, there's no sound. We can't see sound waves, but they're a little like ripples in water - only in three dimensions not two. The speed at which sound waves travel depends on the **density** and **compressibility** of the medium. So, vibrations travel faster through solids and liquids than gases. Sound reception can be improved in many ways: by using cones to funnel vibrations into the ear; using the bony part of the head behind the ear to conduct vibrations; or by reflecting sound.

You will need

A large, ticking alarm clock; a box; a selection of items from Jane's kitchen including: large and small, empty plastic drinks bottles, some with the bottoms cut off and any sharp edges sealed in tape. Sheets of paper, aluminium foil, acetate, cardboard, cocoa tins and yoghurt pots (some with holes punched in the bottoms and sharp edges sealed with tape) large and small empty jam jars; string; lengths of rubber tubing (home brewing kits are a good source); parabolic mirrors; craft knives/scissors; sticky tape.

Safety Remind children never to push objects into their inner ear: this can cause permanent damage.
If you allow the children to use craft knives, firstly show them how to use one safely and then supervise them closely.

Preparation
Place the ticking alarm clock inside the box; try to make it look mysterious.

Discussion and research
● Ask the children to stand at one end of the room, or at the end of a long table. Stand at the other end of the room/table and quietly tap the floor or table top. How well can the children hear the tapping?
● Ask them to cup their hands over their ears and repeat the experiment. *Does the tapping sound the same? How does the tapping sound if you place your ear to the ground/table?*
● Explain that sound waves can be **amplified** and **reflected**. They also travel differently through different mediums. *How can we use this knowledge to help Jane?*

Obtaining evidence
● Show the children a selection of items from Jane's kitchen.
● Together, discuss ideas for 'devices' which may help to amplify or reflect sound.
● You may want to demonstrate some of the ideas below before encouraging the children to experiment for themselves.

● Ideas to try:
Make hearing trumpets out of a variety of materials such as rolled up paper, card or acetate. Experiment with trumpets of different lengths and 'bells' of different sizes. Try lining the bells with foil to reflect sound. Test how trumpet shapes work compared to tube shapes.
Make a stethoscope by cutting the bottom off a plastic drinks bottle and stretching a length of rubber tubing over the neck end.
Construct a 'mobile phone' using two cocoa tins, with a length of string attached through the bottom of each tin. Place one end on the

box and the other over the ear. (Vibrations travelling down the string should be amplified by the tin.) Compare results with yoghurt pot telephones and taut/loose string. (Flexible materials will dampen vibrations.) Place empty jam jars, plastic bottles (empty or filled with water) and inflated balloons against the box and use them as a medium to listen through.
Make a parabolic reflector, coated with foil (or use a parabolic mirror) to reflect sound waves. Sounds should be louder at the 'focus point' between the reflector and the box.

Drawing together
● Round up by challenging the children to demonstrate their most successful listening device(s).
● Compare how well each performs, then work out a 'sound scale' and give each device a score, depending on how loud the object in the box sounds.
● Finally, work together to decide which device was the most successful. Can the children work out why?

Support
Help the children draw labelled diagrams showing their finished listening device.

Extension
Encourage the children to pack the box with a variety of different materials to discover which material blocks sound most effectively.

Scientific language
density - the 'compactness' of an object
compressibility- how easily a substance can be squeezed into a smaller volume
amplify - make stronger/louder
reflect - when light, sound or other particles are 'thrown back'

Up periscope!

Setting the context

During her last assignment, Super Spy Jane Blond found herself in a tricky spot. She had followed Dr Maybee to a hotel, where the evil villainess was meeting a double-agent. Jane didn't want to be recognised, so she had to sit with her back to the Doctor. The problem was how could she get a good look at the double-agent without turning round and being spotted herself? Luckily, when the waiter brought her a pot of tea, she was able to reflect on the situation...

The problem

How can we use reflected light to make a working spy 'scope?

Objectives

To learn that some materials block light causing shadows, and that some materials reflect light.
To know that light travels from a light source.

Background information

Like sound, light travels in waves, like ripples in a pond. When light hits a surface, it may be **absorbed**, refracted or reflected. What happens depends on the surface it encounters. Some materials absorb all light and will look black to the observer. Some materials bend (refract) light. This can be seen when we place a ruler in a jar of water. How much light is refracted depends on the material it passes through. With reflective materials, almost all light bounces back, just like a ball hitting a wall. If the reflective surface is completely flat then the image looks exactly like the original - although it's always reversed, left to right.

You will need

Per group: sheet of foam card; two (50mm x 20mm) rectangular mirrors; double-sided sticky tape; scissors/craft knife; protractor; metal ruler; pencil; fake 'spy-style' beard/glasses (optional); photocopiable pages 92 and 93.

Note: although 50mm x 20mm mirrors work best, the dimensions of the periscope can be adapted to fit almost any sized mirrors. The only fixed measurement is that the mirrors need to be angled at 45° to work.

Preparation

A mock-up of the scene from Jane's story: set two tables for tea (one behind the other) using shiny, metal tea services.
You may also wish to prepare some periscope parts prior to the lesson as some children may well find the activity quite difficult, particularly lower Key Stage 2.

Discussion and research

● We start this activity with a little espionage! Set out the tables for tea and ask for three volunteers - Jane Blond, the villainous Dr Maybee and the elusive double-agent. Sit Jane with her back to Dr Maybee and the double-agent.
● What Jane needs is eyes in the back of her head so she can see the double-agent without being seen herself! Encourage children to speculate how this might be possible.
● Ask them to look carefully at what's on the table before discussing how light is reflected from certain surfaces.

Obtaining evidence

● As we've seen, we can use mirrors and

other reflective surfaces to see behind us. They can also help us to peek round corners and over the top of walls (or carefully positioned newspapers!), using a device called a periscope.

● Some of the children may own periscopes, or have seen them used in films. If so, invite them to share their knowledge before demonstrating how our own spy 'scope can be made.

1. Cut out two pieces of foam card (A & B), 200mm long x 50mm wide.
2. Cut out two pieces of foam card (C & D), 225mm long x 37mm wide.
3. Cut four supports for the mirrors (E) - using a 45° isosceles triangle, where the two shortest edges measure 17.7mm.
4. Using double-sided tape, place two mirror supports on the top corners of cards A & B. Position them so the hypotenuse of the triangles form an angled slope for the mirrors to sit on.

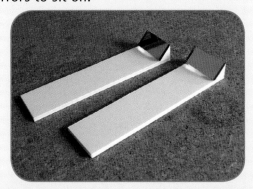

5. Place double-sided tape on the back of the mirrors and stick to each support. Place strips of double-sided tape on each of C & D's long edges.

6. Assemble the periscope by sticking one of the long edges of Card A to Card C so that the mirror is on the inside.

7. Stick the long edge of Card B to the other side of Card C, ensuring that the mirror is at the opposite end. Complete by fixing Card D in place.

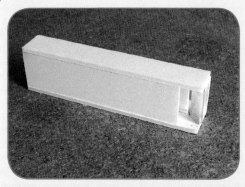

● Finally, encourage the children to make their own periscopes, using photocopiable page 92 as a template. They'll need to be particularly accurate when measuring and cutting, as only carefully constructed 'scopes will work.

Drawing together
● Ask the children to discuss what they've learnt about reflection from the story and from building a periscope. *How are the metallic tea service and the periscope the same/different? What other objects can we name that reflect light? What other ways can light be affected?*
● Round up by inviting children to complete copies of the photocopiable page 93.

Support
Copy the template from photocopiable page 92 onto tracing paper to make the construction of the periscope easier.

Extension
Ask the children to make their own periscopes by noting down the procedure before drawing up their own templates.

Scientific language
absorb - take in

Must dot-dot, dash-dash

Setting the context

Jane often flicks through the pages of *The Super Spy Handbook*, which was written by one of the most famous (but slightly crazy) spies of all, KP Knutt-Nibbler. The Handbook is required reading at spy school and, even now, Jane often finds an interesting article that she hadn't spotted before, such as the one that shows how to send messages using just a torch battery, a few lengths of wire, a paperclip and two drawing pins. Jane's not convinced that it really works.

The problem

Can we really send messages using a torch battery and a few everyday items?

To represent circuits using drawings and symbols.

Background information

Batteries are electro-chemical cells that convert chemical energy into electrical energy. Inside are two terminals - the negative anode and the positive cathode. These are separated by an electrolyte solution through which **ions** can move. By connecting the terminals, we make a circuit. The result is an electric current caused by a flow of positive ions from the anode to the cathode, and negative ions from the cathode to the anode. To send messages using our home-made telegraph, we simply turn this current on or off using the paper clip as a switch. Centuries before text messaging, telegraphs used this technique to produce long or short 'clicks' (called dashes and dots), which could then be translated into English.

You will need

An enlarged copy of photocopiable page 94. Per group: a sheet of Morse code; 4.5v battery with flat terminal connections; 50cm light-weight, insulated wire; miniature 6v

Objectives

To construct simple circuits to make electrical devices work.

buzzer*; metal paper clip; two metal drawing pins; cork floor tile.

Safety Although low-voltage batteries, like the ones we're using for this experiment, are safe, children should be reminded that electricity is dangerous and can kill.

* Minature buzzers and suitable wire can be bought from DIY and specialist electrical stores such as Maplin (www.maplin.co.uk).

Preparation
Using wire cutters, cut two 25cm lengths of light-weight, insulated wire for each group and carefully strip 5cm of insulation from each end.

Discussion and research
● *How many methods of communication can you think of?* Include letter writing and talking, as well as e-mailing and instant messaging. *How do these methods of communication compare to texting?* (Are they as fast, more personal or more fun?)
● Texting may be a modern invention but long before there were mobile phones, people could still send each other messages, fairly quickly, using telegraph machines.
● Explain that, using telegraphs, messages could be sent from one machine to another, across any distance, as long as there was a wire connection between the two. (Home-made telegraphs are simpler but the principles are the same.)
● Tell the children that they are going to test the diagram from *The Super Spy Handbook* to see if they can make their own telegraphs to send each other secret messages.

Obtaining evidence
● Pin up a copy of the photocopiable sheet for reference. Invite children to examine it carefully, then choose their equipment and set up their machines based on what they see in the diagram.
● Encourage each group to test out various designs before completing their machine.
● For best results, children should ensure that: They always connect positive to

negative terminals.

All wires are firmly attached to the battery terminals and each of the drawing pins. The distance between each drawing pin is slightly shorter than the length of the paper clip.
The paper clip, which acts as a switch, is bent upwards slightly, so that the current can be turned on by pushing down. This is just like a transmission key on a real telegraph machine.
● Finally, ask each group to take it in turns to use their finished machines to send short Morse code messages for others to 'decode'.

Drawing together
● Round up by asking the children to discuss how well they think their telegraphs performed and how easy it was to send messages by telegraph compared to modern methods of communication. *Did it matter which wires were connected to which terminals? What part did the battery play in our circuit? What was the job of the switch? If we added a more powerful buzzer, would we need a more powerful battery? Why?*
● Finally, ask the children to write up their experiment as a page from *The Super Spy Handbook*.

Support
As a follow-up activity, help the children apply the same principals to create simple circuits that light up bulbs.

Extension
Challenge the children to investigate series and parallel circuits by adding additional buzzers and/or batteries.

Scientific language
ion - an atom which has lost or gained electrons

Secret messages

Setting the context

Jane suspects that her e-mail is being tampered with! Somehow, Jane believes, the ingenious Dr Maybee has managed to work out a way to intercept her mission reports to the Secret Service boss, 'P'. So Jane has decided to deliver her latest report by hand. Just to make sure that no-one except P will be able to read it, Jane plans to write it in invisible ink, but she needs some help to test out some recipes.

The problem

Which recipe for 'invisible ink' is the best?

Objectives

To describe changes that occur when materials are mixed.
To know that when we burn materials the result is often the formation of a new material.

Background information

Invisible ink really works, and the secret is chemistry. Shop-bought inks often use pairs of chemicals that react with each other: the message is written in one and revealed by applying the other. (Like the grape juice and baking soda recipe.) The best home-made recipes use 'acidic' solutions which weaken parts of the paper. When the paper is heated, the weaker parts burn faster, revealing the message. Milk or other organic substances are also effective. Although they don't damage the paper they still burn/discolour faster than the paper itself. 'Black light' inks and paints work on a different principle, using **UV pigments** that are only visible under black light.

You will need

Ingredients to make a selection of test 'inks' including: any pale citrus juice (lemon works especially well) vinegar; apple juice; baking soda; grape juice; milk (or drinks containing whey powder); sugar; water; corn starch; cold tea; clear herbal shampoos; beakers; desk lamp fitted with a 100 watt bulb or a clothes iron; UV black ink and black light bulb (optional).
Per group: dip pens or cotton buds; white paper; aprons and gloves; selection of test inks; spoons/stirring rods.

Safety Although all of these test inks are made from natural ingredients, check with parents/carers for food allergies before beginning the activity and take appropriate precautions.

● A wide-range of ready-made 'invisible'/'vanishing' inks are available from craft stores, stationers and home-security specialists. Look out for 'black light' aerosols, 'glow paints' and Heribin's Invisible Ink, which works on a similar principle to home-made ink.

Preparation

Prepare labelled beakers containing the ink ingredients.

Discussion and research

● Read out Jane's problem and together discuss the concept of invisible ink. *Is there such a thing as invisible ink? How can it be made? How might it work?* Children who are fans of *Harriet the Spy* or the Alex Rider stories may have some interesting contributions to make to the discussion!

● Explain briefly how some invisible inks work before handing out a selection of ingredients for children/groups to test.

Obtaining evidence

● Challenge the children to test out a variety of potential inks. Before they begin, agree ways to ensure that their experiments are as accurate and fair as possible. For example, always using the same type of paper and pen for each test; deciding how much ink to use for each test and how long the paper should be left to dry.

● For best results be sparing with the ink and write carefully using a dip pen or the tip of a cotton bud.

● Allow the paper to dry thoroughly before heating.

● To reveal messages, place the paper under an ordinary desk lamp fitted with a 100 watt bulb. Leave at least 12cm between the paper and the lamp and watch carefully to ensure the paper doesn't burn. Alternatively, papers can be heated using a cool iron.

● Ideas to test:

Compare fresh and bottled citrus juices. Make up sugar water solutions of different concentrations and compare the results.

Test fresh and powdered milk. Powdered milk can also be made into solutions of varying concentrations.

Mix baking soda with water 1:1 and use the solution to write messages. Leave to dry and then reveal by painting over with grape juice.

Drawing together

● List in a chart all the criteria for good invisible ink such as, 'easy to make', 'invisible when dry', 'easy to write with', 'produces clear messages'. Then encourage the children to demonstrate their best ink(s).

● Give each ink a score, using the criteria before deciding on the most effective recipe.

Support

Pre-prepare some 'inks' for the children to try. These can be placed in small beakers and labelled accordingly.

Extension

Invite the children to write up their experiment as a report to Jane's boss, 'P'.

Scientific language

invisible - any object which can't be seen

UV - meaning ultra violet. UV waves are shorter than the waves at the violet end of the visible light spectrum and are usually invisible

pigment - a natural or manufactured substance which gives colour to objects

All in a day's work

Setting the context

Jane Blond has spent most of the day on the trail of her arch-nemesis, Dr Maybee. Using the latest digital surveillance equipment, Jane has been able to make a detailed record to show the Doctor's movements during 24 hours. Unfortunately, she forgot to set the time on her digital camera, so now that she's printed out all of the images, she has no way of telling exactly what happened when. Or has she?

The problem

What are the 'periodic changes' that happen over the course of an average day?

Objectives

To learn that science is about finding the answers to questions through observation, investigation and evaluation.

To know that science is about thinking creatively to explain how things work.

To know that day and night are related to the spin of the Earth.

To understand how months and years are related to the orbits of the Earth and Moon.

Background information

Our planet is constantly on the move. Not only does it **orbit** the Sun, but it also rotates on its own **axis**. It takes approximately 24 hours to complete one full rotation. Although the position of the Sun in the sky appears to change during the day, it's really Earth that is moving. It takes around 365 days for the Earth to complete one full orbit of the Sun. As our planet moves, different parts of the surface receive more or less sunlight, creating seasons. However, as the Earth isn't completely round, the amount of daylight we receive changes over the year too, as the Earth tilts on its axis towards one pole then another.

You will need

A copy of the photograph taken outside the school; a globe that can be spun on its axis; a desk lamp or torch; notebooks; access to digital cameras; video recorders; photocopiable page 95.

Safety Children should be taught never to look directly at the Sun or even the Moon. To do so can cause permanent and irreversible eye damage.

Preparation

Take a photograph outside the school; ideally the image should give lots of clues to the time of day. If a globe is unavailable then make one by covering an inflated balloon in papier mâché. Allow to dry completely before painting and then push a knitting needle through the centre, so that the paper planet can be spun on its own axis.

Discussion and research

● Begin by asking the children: *Why do we have night and day? Why do we have seasons?*

● Remind the children about Jane's problem

Photos © Stock.xchng.

and ask them to suggest how she might be able to tell what time of day it is in each photograph.

● Draw out the fact that we can use visual clues, such as the height of the Sun in the sky, the amount of daylight we can see and the angles of the shadows on the ground.

● Together draw up a list of potential 'clues' that Jane could use to sort out the order of her surveillance photographs.

Obtaining evidence

● Using their list of clues, ask the children to work out what time of day is shown in our photograph.

● They'll need to use both observation and deduction. For example, if there are children in the playground, then we know it's break time. *Can we narrow the time down further by looking at the height of the Sun in the sky or the angle of the shadows on the ground? Can we tell what season it is or what the weather is like? Do the clothes the children are wearing give us any clues? Can we see any leaves on the trees?*

● Hand out copies of the photocopiable sheet and invite children to plan their own photographs/videos showing 'A day in the life of our school'.

● They will need to plan each image/scene carefully to give the viewer clues to the time of day
the image was captured.

● Finally, depending on available resources, help the children to make their photograph/

video records using either still photographs, moving images, sketches or a combination of all three.

Drawing together

● Round up by inviting the children to discuss how easy/difficult it was to capture an image that gives the viewer all the necessary clues they need.

● Finally, ask children to share their photographs/videos with the rest of the group.

Support

If necessary, use the globe and desk lamp to explain how the Earth spins on its axis and orbits the Sun, and how this affects the amount of light and heat we receive.

Extension

As a longer-term project, record 'A year in the life of our school' taking just a few images every month in the same location to show the changing seasons.

Scientific language

orbit - the path a planet takes around the Sun

axis - an imaginary line around which the Earth spins

Fantastic forensics

Setting the context
When Jane arrived at Secret Service HQ this morning, she found the place in uproar. During the night, one of Dr Maybee's henchmen sneaked past security, and stole some top secret files. As they cunningly kept their faces hidden, they can't be identified from the security camera pictures. However, Jane believes that there are only three people who have the skills to pull off this sort of break-in. All she needs is enough evidence to work out which one.

The problem
What evidence do you need to identify the mystery visitor?

Objectives
To learn that science is about finding the answers to questions through observation, investigation and evaluation.
To know that science is about thinking creatively to explain how things work.

Background information
Forensics is the application of science to solve crime. Sherlock Holmes was probably one of the first fictional characters to use this scientific method to collect evidence and track down suspects. Yet, real-life forensics dates back to Archimedes (287-212 BC) who was able to prove that a crown was not made of gold by testing its buoyancy. Today, television shows like *CSI* have made forensics a popular science. There are many branches of forensics specialising in specific types of evidence such as ballistics, which deals with firearms and forensic chemistry, which concerns explosives and poisons.

You will need
Per group: dossiers on each suspect; magnifying glasses; tweezers; evidence bags; marker pen and labels to 'tag' finds; Plaster of Paris; cardboard; jam jars and vinegar for chromatography; talc and/or cocoa powder; soft make-up brush; clear tape; digital camera.

Preparation
Invent three fictional suspects and prepare 'dossiers' on each, describing their appearance and habits. Include a set of finger-prints for each suspect, plus hand-writing samples, all written by different people in different inks. Add information such as 'always wears trainers'; 'wears red

nail varnish'; 'has blond hair'; 'likes tartan'; 'smokes'; 'lives near a forest'; 'drinks cola'. At the scene of the crime, plant fingerprints and other items of 'trace evidence'. Include a hand-written note to Jane from the suspect, a footprint - anything, in short, that will link the intruder to one of the suspects in the dossiers. Children will then have to determine if the evidence you plant belongs to Suspect X, Y or Z.

Discussion and research

● Read out Jane's story and challenge children to suggest ways of identifying the suspect. Note down their ideas, including anything that they may have seen on TV crime shows, before going on to discuss a little about how real-life forensics works.

● Finally, split the children into teams of Forensic Investigators and ask them to work together to gather evidence.

Obtaining evidence

● During their investigations, children will need to work carefully and be aware of where they stand and what they touch in case they disturb evidence.

● Encourage them to take detailed photographs/make sketches of the scene before their investigation and of each piece of evidence found.

● They may also like to map out the crime scene and divide it into plots which can be more easily searched. (Remind them of the work they completed from pages 36-37.)

● Collect trace evidence:
Hand out magnifying glasses, tweezers and evidence bags (use skills learned from pages 34-35).
Conduct detailed searches for lost buttons, lengths of hair, fibres from clothes, cigarette butts, leaves, muddy footprints and so on.

● Dust for fingerprints:
Use soft make up brushes to dust surfaces with talc or cornstarch to reveal fingerprints. (Cocoa powder can be used on dark surfaces.)
Fingerprints can then be collected, using strips of clear tape, and fixed to sheets of dark card.

● Handwriting analysis:
Compare the handwriting in the note with the samples in the dossiers.
If results are inconclusive, then chromatography can be used to match the ink on the note to the ink on the samples, using the skills learned on pages 30-31.
Hidden messages may also be discovered by testing papers for invisible ink or by rubbing them with a soft pencil to reveal the imprint of anything that was written on the sheet above.

● Make plaster casts:
Make plaster casts of any footprints at the scene.
Measure the depth and circumference of the print (use a piece of string for the circumference).
Cut out a cardboard collar the length of the stringand about twice the depth of the print. Carefully set it into the hole. Make up a batch of Plaster of Paris and pour onto the print. Allow to set and remove, using the collar for leverage.

Drawing together

● Ask each team of Forensic Investigators to appoint a spokesperson to summarise their findings to the rest of the group.

● Then hand out the dossiers and encourage groups to use the evidence they've gathered to identify a 'prime suspect'.

● Conclude by deciding who was Jane's mystery visitor.

Support
Hand out the dossiers before the children begin their investigation.

Extension
Invite the children to write up a report on their findings for Jane's Boss, 'P'. They should list each piece of evidence found and explain how it helped to identify their suspect.

Up periscope! 1

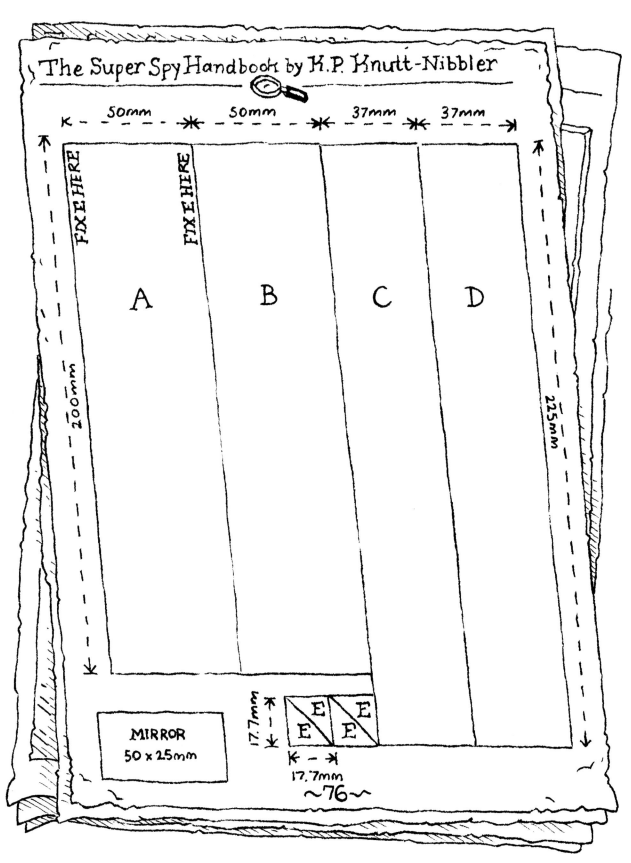

The Super Spy Handbook by K.P. Knutt-Nibbler

50mm · 50mm · 37mm · 37mm

FIXE HERE · FIXE HERE

A · B · C · D

200mm

225mm

MIRROR
50 x 25mm

17.7mm

E E E E

17.7mm

~76~

■ SCHOLASTIC
www.scholastic.co.uk

Up periscope! 2

- Work out how each of these items affect light.

Absorb/Reflect/Refract

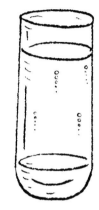

Absorb/Reflect/Refract

Absorb/Reflect/Refract

Absorb/Reflect/Refract

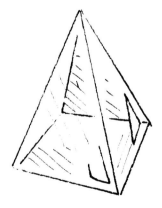

Absorb/Reflect/Refract

Absorb/Reflect/Refract

Teacher's notes: As an additional activity, allow children to view and copy the type of image which they see reflected/refracted in the water, mirror, prism and teapot.

Must dot-dot, dash-dash

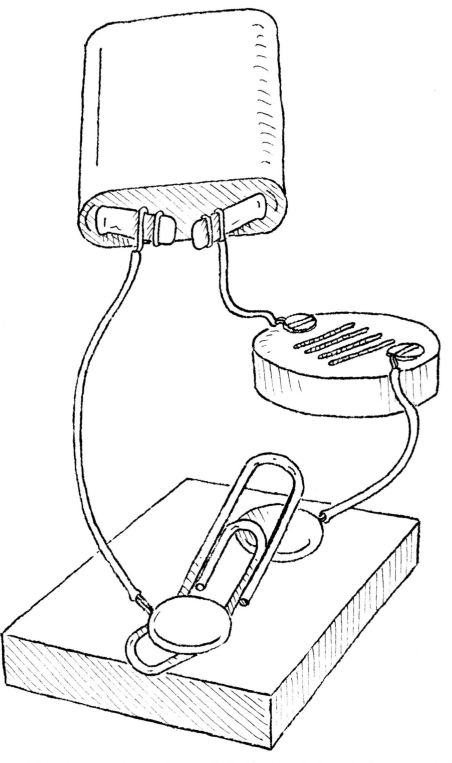

Teacher's notes: This sheet can be used as an individual worksheet, to be correctly labelled, or enlarged for use with whole groups.

All in a day's work

Storyboard

Date: _____

Name: _____

Dialogue: _____
_____
_____

Visual

Storyboard

Date: _____

Name: _____

Dialogue: _____
_____
_____

Visual

Storyboard

Date: _____

Name: _____

Dialogue: _____
_____
_____

Visual

Storyboard

Date: _____

Name: _____

Dialogue: _____
_____
_____

Visual

SCHOLASTIC

In this series:

ISBN 978-0439-94500-4

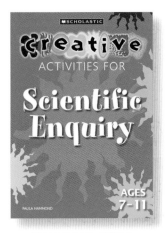

ISBN 978-0439-94501-1

Also available:

ISBN 978-0439-97111-9

ISBN 978-0439-97112-6

ISBN 978-0439-97113-3

ISBN 978-0439-96526-2

ISBN 978-0439-96525-5

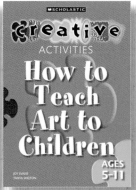

ISBN 978-0439-96524-8

ISBN 978-0439-96556-9

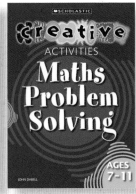

ISBN 978-0439-96570-5

To find out more, call: 0845 603 9091
or visit our website www.scholastic.co.uk